Lecture Notes in Business Information Processing 338

More information about this series at http://www.springer.com/series/7911

Dietmar Winkler · Stefan Biffl
Johannes Bergsmann (Eds.)

Software Quality

The Complexity and Challenges of Software Engineering and Software Quality in the Cloud

11th International Conference, SWQD 2019
Vienna, Austria, January 15–18, 2019
Proceedings

Springer

Editors
Dietmar Winkler (iD)
Vienna University of Technology
Vienna, Austria

Johannes Bergsmann
Software Quality Lab GmbH
Linz, Austria

Stefan Biffl
Vienna University of Technology
Vienna, Austria

ISSN 1865-1348   ISSN 1865-1356   (electronic)
Lecture Notes in Business Information Processing
ISBN 978-3-030-05766-4   ISBN 978-3-030-05767-1   (eBook)
https://doi.org/10.1007/978-3-030-05767-1

Library of Congress Control Number: 2018963974

This Springer imprint is published by the registered company Springer Nature Switzerland AG
The registered company address is: Gewerbestrasse 11, 6330 Cham, Switzerland

Message from the General Chair

The Software Quality Days (SWQD) conference and tools fair started in 2009 and has grown to be the biggest conferences on software quality in Europe with a strong community. The program of the SWQD conference is designed to encompass a stimulating mixture of practical presentations and new research topics in scientific presentations as well as tutorials and an exhibition area for tool vendors and other organizations in the area of software quality.

This professional symposium and conference offer a range of comprehensive and valuable opportunities for advanced professional training, new ideas, and networking with a series of keynote speeches, professional lectures, exhibits, and tutorials.

The SWQD conference is suitable for anyone with an interest in software quality, such as software process and quality managers, test managers, software testers, product managers, agile masters, project managers, software architects, software designers, requirements engineers, user interface designers, software developers, IT managers, release managers, development managers, application managers, and similar roles.

The guiding conference topic of the SWQD 2019 was "The Complexity and Challenges of Software Engineering and Software Quality in the Cloud," as changed product, process, and service requirements, e.g., distributed engineering projects, mobile applications, involvement of heterogeneous disciplines and stakeholders, extended application areas, and new technologies, include new challenges and might require new and adapted methods and tools to support quality assurance activities early.

January 2019   Johannes Bergsmann

Message from the Scientific Program Chair

The 11th Software Quality Days (SWQD) conference and tools fair brought together researchers and practitioners from business, industry, and academia working on quality assurance and quality management for software engineering and information technology. The SWQD conference is one of the largest software quality conferences in Europe.

Over the past years a growing number of scientific contributions were submitted to the SWQD symposium. Starting in 2012 the SWQD symposium included a dedicated scientific program published in scientific proceedings. For the eighth event in the series, we received an overall number of 17 high-quality submissions from researchers across Europe, which were each peer-reviewed by three or more reviewers. Out of these submissions, the editors selected five contributions as full papers, for an acceptance rate of 29%. Further, three short papers, representing promising research directions, were accepted to spark discussions between researchers and practitioners at the conference. This year we had invited two scientific keynote speaker for the scientific program who contributed with two invited papers.

The main topics from academia and industry focused on "Systems and Software Quality Management Methods," "Improvements of Software Development Methods and Processes," "Latest Trends and Emerging Topics in Software Quality," and "Testing and Software Quality Assurance."

This book is structured according to the sessions of the scientific program following the guiding conference topic "The Complexity and Challenges of Software Engineering and Software Quality in the Cloud":

- Multidisciplinary Systems and Software Engineering
- Software Quality and Process Improvement
- Software Testing
- Knowledge Engineering and Machine Learning
- Source Code Analysis
- Software Maintenance

January 2019   Stefan Biffl

Organization

SWQD 2019 was organized by Software Quality Lab GmbH and the Vienna University of Technology, Institute of Information Systems Engineering, Information and Software Engineering Group.

Organizing Committee

General Chair

Johannes Bergsmann   Software Quality Lab GmbH, Austria

Scientific Program Chair

Stefan Biffl   Vienna University of Technology, Austria

Proceedings Chair

Dietmar Winkler   Vienna University of Technology, Austria

Organizing and Publicity Chair

Petra Bergsmann   Software Quality Lab GmbH, Austria

Program Committee

SWQD 2019 established an international committee of well-known experts in software quality and process improvement to peer-review the scientific submissions.

Maria Teresa Baldassarre	University of Bari, Italy
Miklos Biro	Software Competence Center Hagenberg, Austria
Matthias Book	University of Iceland, Iceland
Ruth Breu	University of Innsbruck, Austria
Maya Daneva	University of Twente, The Netherlands
Oscar Dieste	Universidad Politécnica de Madrid, Spain
Frank Elberzhager	Fraunhofer IESE, Germany
Michael Felderer	University of Innsbruck, Austria
Gordon Fraser	University of Sheffield, UK
Nauman Ghazi	Blekinge Institute of Technology, Sweden
Volker Gruhn	University of Duisburg-Essen, Germany
Roman Haas	Technische Universität München, Germany
Jens Heidrich	Fraunhofer IESE, Germany
Frank Houdek	Daimler AG, Germany
Slinger Jansen	Utrecht University, The Netherlands
Marcos Kalinowski	Pontifical Catholic University of Rio de Janeiro, Brazil

Contents

Multi-Disciplinary Systems and Software Engineering

Multi-disciplinary Engineering of Production Systems – Challenges
for Quality of Control Software 3
   Arndt Lüder, Johanna-Lisa Pauly, and Konstantin Kirchheim

Towards a Flexible and Secure Round-Trip-Engineering Process
for Production Systems Engineering with Agile Practices 14
   Dietmar Winkler, Felix Rinker, and Peter Kieseberg

Software Quality and Process Improvement

Relating Verification and Validation Methods to Software Product
Quality Characteristics: Results of an Expert Survey 33
   Isela Mendoza, Marcos Kalinowski, Uéverton Souza,
   and Michael Felderer

Listen to Your Users – Quality Improvement of Mobile Apps Through
Lightweight Feedback Analyses 45
   Simon André Scherr, Frank Elberzhager, and Selina Meyer

Agile Software Process Improvement by Learning from Financial
and Fintech Companies: LHV Bank Case Study 57
   Erki Kilu, Fredrik Milani, Ezequiel Scott, and Dietmar Pfahl

Software Testing

Why Software Testing Fails: Common Pitfalls Observed
in a Critical Smart Metering Project 73
   Stefan Mohacsi and Rudolf Ramler

Knowledge Engineering and Machine Learning

Mixed Reality Applications in Industry: Challenges and Research Areas 95
   Thomas Moser, Markus Hohlagschwandtner, Gerhard Kormann-Hainzl,
   Sabine Pölzlbauer, and Josef Wolfartsberger

Improving Defect Localization by Classifying the Affected Asset
Using Machine Learning 106
   Sam Halali, Miroslaw Staron, Miroslaw Ochodek, and Wilhelm Meding

Source Code Analysis

Benefits and Drawbacks of Representing and Analyzing Source Code
and Software Engineering Artifacts with Graph Databases   125
  *Rudolf Ramler, Georg Buchgeher, Claus Klammer, Michael Pfeiffer,
  Christian Salomon, Hannes Thaller, and Lukas Linsbauer*

Software Maintenance

Evaluating Maintainability Prejudices with a Large-Scale Study
of Open-Source Projects.   151
  Tobias Roehm, Daniel Veihelmann, Stefan Wagner, and Elmar Juergens

Author Index   173

Multi-Disciplinary Systems and Software Engineering

Multi-disciplinary Engineering of Production Systems – Challenges for Quality of Control Software

Arndt Lüder$^{(\boxtimes)}$, Johanna-Lisa Pauly, and Konstantin Kirchheim

Otto-von-Guericke University, Universitätsplatz 2, 39106 Magdeburg, Germany
{arndt.lueder,johanna-lisa.pauly,
konstantin.kirchheim}@ovgu.de

Abstract. Production systems and their inherent control systems are developed within an increasingly multi-disciplinary and increasingly complex engineering process which is, in addition, increasingly interlinked with the other life cycle phases of the production system. Surely this will have consequences for efficiency and correctness of the control system engineering.

Within this paper bordering conditions and challenges of this multi-disciplinary engineering process will be discussed and a centralized data logistics will be presented as one possible mean for handling the identified challenges. Thereby, requirements to the further development in the field of standardized data exchange are discussed possibly supported by software industry.

Keywords: Multi-disciplinary engineering · Production system control Engineering quality and efficiency

1 Motivation

Control systems are an integral part of production systems and, thereby, subject to the same life cycles as the production system and its components themselves. But this production system life cycle is impacted by various factors [1].

Here, special importance needs to be placed on the original intention of the existence of production systems, the production of sellable products. This is indicated in Fig. 1 based on [2].

The main motivation for the development and implementation of the production system is the intention to produce and ship products in an economically reasonable way. Hence, the product development and the product line development are providing the first starting points for the production system life cycle with the definition of the required material and necessary production processes within the Bill of Material and the Bill of Operations. The second starting point is given by the design and test of production methods (and thereby production system resources realizing these production methods) that can be applied to realize the necessary production processes.

Based on these two starting points the production system engineering can initially identify and select appropriate production system resources and can execute the

© Springer Nature Switzerland AG 2019
D. Winkler et al. (Eds.): SWQD 2019, LNBIP 338, pp. 3–13, 2019.
https://doi.org/10.1007/978-3-030-05767-1_1

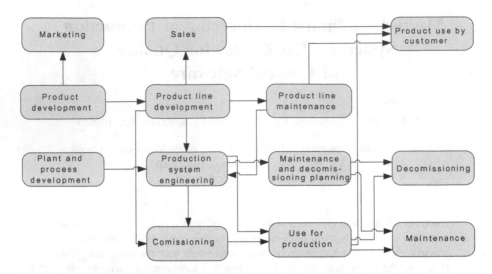

Fig. 1. Interlinked product and production system life cycles (based on [2])

detailed production system engineering afterwards. This detailing process has to result in a complete production system modelling, covering all necessary information and work instructions required to physically realize and ramp-up the production system.

If the production system is in operation, the production orders and the detailed work instructions of product engineering and production system engineering are the foundation of the production system behaviour and its control on the different levels of the automation pyramid [3].

Within all named life cycle phases the control system engineering and application are an integral part. Within the control system engineering, information related to

- the characteristic of the product making process coming from product engineering,
- the structure and behaviour of production system resources coming from plant panning, and
- the structure of the wiring of integrated sensors and actuators from mechanical and electrical engineering of the detailed system planning

are required. This engineering information is the fundamentals of the control engineering covering the configuration of the control devices and the control code programming.

Faulty and incomplete engineering information may lead to unintended results of the engineering, negatively impacting the successful commissioning and economical application of the production system [4]. Thus, the quality of engineering data applied within control system engineering has an essential impact on control engineering quality.

But the necessary data exchange is hampered by the networked structure of the chains of engineering and data processing units within the production system life cycle [5]. As Fig. 2 is depicting, especially within the early phases of the production system life cycle the network of data processing units consists of a huge set of engineering tools applied within the different engineering domains to take engineering decisions and to create engineering artefacts. They are optimally tailored towards the specific engineering activities and their design decisions as for example identified in [6]. But, following their development history, they are not or insufficiently tailored to the necessary information exchange between engineering tools, if at all.

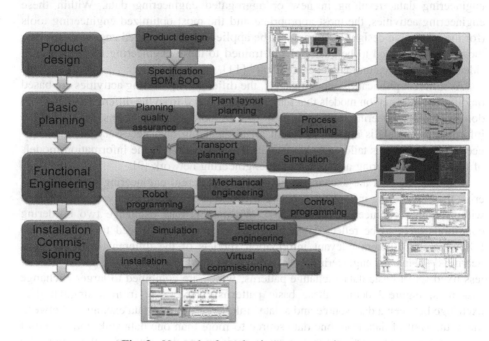

Fig. 2. Network of production system engineering

One starting point for the minimization of problems related to faulty and incomplete engineering data has been presented in [5]. It is based on the application of appropriate production system architectures and the development of engineering networks adapted to them. Here especially the mechatronic engineering has gained importance. But this concept is not applicable in all use cases, as in certain use cases special system architectures and engineering networks, have been developed following legal regulations, industrial needs, and company decisions.

The aim of this paper is to sketch bordering conditions and challenges of the engineering data exchange arising in engineering networks and to discuss means provided by information sciences to cope with them to realize an efficient and fault free plant (and thereby) control system engineering.

2 Structure of Engineering Networks

The engineering process of production systems establishes a hierarchical network of engineering phases and engineering activities [7, 8]. Within the engineering activities of these networks the engineering decisions will be taken based on the available engineering data, resulting in new or aggregated engineering data. Within these engineering activities, the most appropriate and the most optimized engineering tools (for the respective design decisions) will be applied by the involved engineers. Hence, these engineers need to be qualified and trained to these engineering tools they considering as their "natural engineering habit" [11].

As different publications document [1], the different engineering activities are based on different information models that historically emerged from the different engineering domains and engineering tools with their specific bordering conditions. Each of these information models is able to represent all engineering data necessary for the engineering activities it is tailored to but usually not compatible to the information models of the other engineering activities of the engineering network [9].

Engineering data are exchanged between the different engineering activities covering the engineering information created within one engineering activity and required within another engineering activity [10]. Within this data exchange two bordering conditions have to be reflected. At first, the exchanged data need to be converted following the different relevant information models of the different involved engineering domains and engineering tools. At second, the data exchange follows a more or less fixed set of basic data exchange patterns, which are combined to larger exchange structures. Figure 3 depicts these basic patterns. They range from a singular data exchange between a data source and a data sink, over multiple data exchanges between them, the split of data from one data source to more than one data sink, the merge of data coming from more than one data sources within one data sink up to the data cyclic data exchange between to partners which act in this pattern as both sink and source of data.

Summarizing modern engineering networks can be considered as systems of interacting engineering activities exchanging engineering data covering engineering information. These data exchanges follow different patterns where engineering data need to be converted. In general they form a multidisciplinary model and information system, containing the control engineering as one engineering discipline.

3 Challenges Within Engineering Networks

The described structure of engineering networks results in a set of challenges to be handled within the efficient and fault free production system can control system engineering.

3.1 Engineering Habit

The engineering habit is considered as the usual bordering and execution condition of an engineering activity [11, 12]. Thus it is based on the usually applied engineering

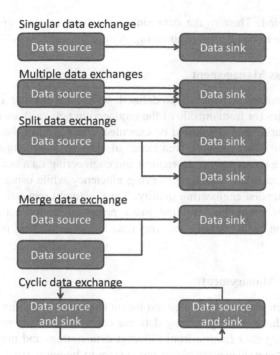

Fig. 3. Basic data exchange patterns

tools, information models, engineering methods and procedures the executing engineer is accustomed and trained to. Their application is supporting the engineering efficiency and quality of the involved engineers.

As the engineers are tailored to these tools, information models and methods/procedures, the involved engineers are usually not interested in any change to the bordering and execution conditions of an engineering activity, i.e. to change their engineering habit. Especially changes with respect to the applied tools and information models are usually rejected and can trigger counter-actions of the involved engineers, possibly leading to a reduced engineering efficiency and quality.

3.2 Change Management

Reacting on the increasing system complexity, the engineering within the different engineering activities is executed incrementally, i.e. step by step. Hence, not only the final engineering results will be exchanged with the subsequent engineering activities, but also intermediate results with different degree of completeness and correctness. In addition, the engineering networks are branched and partially cyclic.

Therefore, engineering activities acting as data sink have to import engineering data multiple times from different data sources. Within this import they have to able to identify the changes of the overall engineering results, i.e. they have to be able to distinguish whether an information on an engineering object is new, changed, unchanged or deleted. Thereby the data sink is enabled to react appropriately and enable the engineer to handle the engineering data in the right way.

3.3   Completeness Management

To execute engineering activities a predefined set of engineering data from prior engineering activities (or from outside of the engineering network) are required. At the moment an engineering activity should be executed, and not all of the required data is available, there are three possible reactions of the involved engineer: wait, use approximations or average values, or request the engineering data actively.

To wait will lead to a reduced engineering efficiency while using approximations may violate the intended engineering quality. Thus, actively requesting the necessary engineering data is preferable. But the main precondition for actively requesting missing information is to identify missing data as well as their potential sources uniquely.

3.4   Consistency Management

Assuming that all engineering data required for an engineering activity are available, it is not guaranteed that these engineering data are consistent. This is mainly due to the fact, that engineering data emerge from different data sources and may have different degrees of completeness/development of the system to be engineered.

Therefore, the possibility of contradicting engineering information has to be considered. To address this challenge, it shall be possible to model and evaluate consistency and semantical correctness of engineering data with respect to natural laws, technical conditions, etc. as consistency rules within the engineering data model.

3.5   Migration of Engineering Networks

The challenge, finally to be named, emerges from the volatility of engineering networks. Following the requirements defined within the Industrie 4.0 approach [13], it has to be assumed that engineering activities (and with them engineering tools and possibly engineering disciplines) will join the engineering network or leave it. In addition engineering tools can be exchanged within the different engineering activities (following the needs of the project execution or customer requirements).

Hence, it shall be possible to incrementally adjust the engineering data exchange within the engineering networks from existing structures and technologies to the intended ones to ensure an efficient and fault free production system as well as control system engineering [14].

4 Solution Approach

In this section, a centralized data logistics with intelligent tool adapters is proposed as a solution candidate for the challenges discussed in the previous chapters. It shall ensure the efficient and fault free engineering of production systems and (thereby) of control systems and reflect the five named challenges.

4.1 Centralised Data Logistics

The main aim of the centralized data logistics is to maintain and provide an integrated, consistent and complete overall model of the production system to be engineered (including its control system) over the complete life cycle of the production system. Therefore, this overall model shall be detailed step by step within the engineering phase and adapted (if necessary) to its physical occurrence during installation, ramp-up and use phases. If it is installed (even if only partially), it can act as a relay station for the engineering data exchange between engineering data sources and sinks.

Based on the overall model within the centralized data logistics, the following functionalities can be implemented:

- Change management can be realized by providing and maintaining information on model versions and releases, also covering information on successfully finished engineering phases or information addressing system states like "as designed", "as build", or "as maintained". In addition the amount of changes between two versions can be indicated by a data status like "new", "changed", "unchanged" or "deleted".
- Completeness management can be realized by defining identifiers for the necessary amount of data required for an engineering activity and an evaluation method based on these identifiers enabling the evaluation of the degree of completeness related to a given intended data set.
- Consistency management can be realized by modeling and evaluating consistency rules integrated in the overall engineering data model including the identification of possible failure sources.

To enable these functions the centralized data logistics requires capabilities to import, manage, analyze, and export data and to support different views on the engineering data. This view support shall enable the reflection of different engineering disciplines and different engineering tools involved in the engineering network.

At this point, it shall be emphasized that a centralized data logistic does not need to be a central data storage. The only requirement is a data storing architecture that contains a complete navigable and analyzable data model with a central entrance point.

4.2 Flexible Adapters

The flexible tool adapters as intelligent tool interfaces (or interfaces to other data processing systems like model generators) are intended to support the data transfer between engineering tools and centralized data logistics. They are responsible for the necessary transformation of the tool dependent data models to the data model applied within the centralized data logistics and vice versa.

The flexible tool adapters enable to cope with the following challenges:

- Decoupling of the different engineering habits of involved engineers between each other and towards the centralized data logistics.
- Enabling of extensions and migration scenarios by using the possibility of sequentially realizing tool adapters as well as their design, depending to the intended application cases.

The resulting architecture of the data logistics is depicted in Fig. 4.

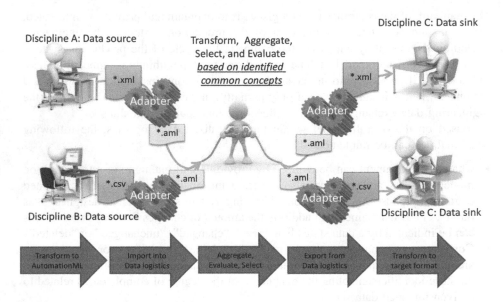

Fig. 4.   Data logistics within engineering networks

5   Preconditions for Solution

The described solution approach requires some modelling related and data management related capabilities of the intended data logistics.

5.1   Modelling Capabilities

The architecture of the centralized data logistics requires the possibility to integrate the different tool specific data models within a common data model. Finally, this data model needs to be implemented. As shown in [14] AutomationML can be applied as technological (especially data exchange format related) foundation for this implementation. It provides sufficient modelling capabilities. In addition it provides means for representation of views and means for incremental enrichment.

It is assumed that there are two types of AutomationML based data models. The first type represents the data models of the individual tool interfaces. Therefore, it is engineering discipline and engineering tool dependent and engineering view and project role specific. This type of AutomationML model enables the representation of the relevant concepts of the related disciplines/tools and their properties and relations (including hierarchy relations). Therefore is needs to be visible for the individual engineers within a project to identify and use their engineering data.

The second type of AutomationML data models originates from the data model of the centralized data logistics. It is established as the conceptual union of all involved discipline/tool specific data models. Thus, it enables the representation of all relevant concepts with properties and relations of the complete engineering process. This data model is designed by combination of all data models of the first type in an step-by-step approach were conflicting model properties (for example conflicting hierarchies of modelled objects) are represented as parallel relations. This will avoid problems with view specific properties related to consistency. Therefore, does not have to be visible to the "normal" engineers, as only specialized data management engineers will develop and main it.

5.2 Data Management Capabilities

With respect to data management the architecture of the centralized data logistics requires capabilities related to versioning of engineering data. Changes within the data model emerging from the import of data within the data logistics (coming from an arbitrary engineering tool) need to be identifiable. It is not sufficient to just identify that an object/data point has been changed, but has it be examined whether it has been added, altered or removed and by whom? The resulting version history of related engineering data needs to be stored in an integrated way, managed, evaluated qualitatively, and imported and exported based on various data views.

The data management itself requires the ability to define and apply views on the data and some sort of data access management based on the views, for example. Within this data access management, permissions of reading and writing needs to be assigned, for example based on engineering roles and views.

Beyond the completeness management requires the capability to model explicitly the sources and sinks of engineering data at each relevant data point which can be realised by using roles and refSemantics within AutomationML.

There exist several approaches for such a data management based on AutomationML [15–17].

6 Conclusions

The increasing complexity of products and production systems and their intended networking has resulted in an increasing complexity of the information management within system engineering (and the control engineering within). The required efficiency and correctness of the engineering is even more increasing this complexity.

Within this paper bordering conditions for the data exchange within engineering networks have been derived following this complexity increase. Thereby, the challenges of engineering habits, change management, completeness management, consistency management, and engineering network migration have been derived. These challenges need to be addressed by modern engineering networks exploiting IT capabilities.

To tackle these challenges a concept for an architecture has been presented, providing a centralised engineering data logistics with flexible adapters to integrate engineering tools. Within this architecture AutomationML can be exploited as appropriate technological foundation.

The further development and prototypical implementation of the presented architecture are the main aims of the Christian Doppler Lab for improvement of security and quality of production system engineering (see www.sqi.at). Within this research and development project researchers from Technical University Vienna and from Otto.-von-Guericke University Magdeburg are cooperating with industrial partners to improve, implement and test the named architecture within different industrial application cases.

Similar aims are considered within the INTEGRATE project (see https://forschung-sachsen-anhalt.de/project/integrate-offene-dienste-plattform-durchgaengiges-20720) researching the application of an AutomationML based central data storage to be applied within the complete life cycle of a production system.

Both projects shall provide a proof of concept for the practical applicability of the presented architecture and their benefits related to the realization of an efficient and fault free production system and thereby control system engineering process.

Acknowledgement. The financial support one the one hand by the Christian Doppler Research Association, the Austrian Federal Ministry for Digital and Economic Affairs and the National Foundation for Research, Technology and Development and on the other hand by the German Federal Ministry of economic Affairs and Energy within the PAICE program are gratefully acknowledged.

References

1. Biffl, S., Lüder, A., Gerhard, D. (eds.): Multi-Disciplinary Engineering for Cyber-Physical Production Systems. Springer, Cham (2017). https://doi.org/10.1007/978-3-319-56345-9. ISBN 978-3-319-56344-2
2. VDI/VDE: Industrie 4.0 -Wertschöpfungsketten, VDI/VDE Gesellschaft Mess- und Automatisierungs-technik, Status Report, April 2014
3. Vogel-Heuser, B.: Herausforderungen und Anforderungen aus Sicht der IT und der Automatisierungstechnik. In: Vogel-Heuser, B., Bauernhansl, T., ten Hompel, M. (eds.) Handbuch Industrie 4.0 Bd.4. SRT, pp. 33–44. Springer, Heidelberg (2017). https://doi.org/10.1007/978-3-662-53254-6_2
4. Strahilov, A., Hämmerle, H.: Engineering workflow and software tool chains of automated production systems. In: Biffl, S., Lüder, A., Gerhard, D. (eds.) Multi-Disciplinary Engineering for Cyber-Physical Production Systems, pp. 207–234. Springer, Cham (2017). https://doi.org/10.1007/978-3-319-56345-9_9
5. Lüder, A., Schmidt, N.: Challenges of mechatronical engineering of production systems: an automation system engineering view. In: Ghezzi, L., Hömberg, D., Landry, C. (eds.) Math for the Digital Factory. MI, vol. 27, pp. 93–114. Springer, Cham (2017). https://doi.org/10.1007/978-3-319-63957-4_5

6. Hell, K.: Methoden der projektübergreifenden Wie-derverwendung im Anlagenentwurf, Ph. D. thesis, Otto-v.-Guericke University, Magdeburg, Germany, March 2018
7. Lindemann, U.: Methodische Entwicklung technischer Produkte. Springer, Heidelberg (2007). https://doi.org/10.1007/978-3-540-37451-0
8. Lüder, A., Foehr, M., Hundt, L., Hoffmann, M., Langer, Y., Frank, S.: Aggregation of engineering processes regarding the mechatronic approach. In: 16th IEEE International Conference on Emerging Technologies and Factory Automation (ETFA 2011), Proceedings-CD, Toulouse, France, September 2011
9. Diedrich, Ch., Lüder, A., Hundt, L.: Bedeutung der Interoperabilität bei Entwurf und Nutzung von automatisierten Produktionssystemen. at –Automatisierungstechnik **59**(7), 426–438 (2011)
10. Wolff, D., Hundt, L., Dreher, S.: Requirements on the engineering of advanced standby strategies in automobile production. In: 11th Global Conference on Sustainable Manufacturing, Proceedings, Berlin, Germany, pp. 165–170, September 2013
11. Kaufmann, U., Pfenning, M.: Was die Produkt- von der Softwareentwicklung lernen kann. In: Tag des Systems Engineering 2014, Proceedings, pp. 329–337. Hanser Verlag
12. Fischer, S.: Agilität, Agile HR Konferenz, Köln, Deutschland, April 2016. http://hr-pioneers. com/wp-content/uploads/2016/04/Hochschule-Pforzheim.pdf
13. Kagermann, H., Wahlster, W., Helbig, J. (eds.) Umsetzungsempfehlungen für das Zukunftsprojekt Industrie 4.0 – Deutschlands Zukunft als Industriestandort sichern, Forschungsunion Wirtschaft und Wissenschaft, Arbeitskreis Industrie 4.0 (2013). https://www.bmbf.de/files/Umsetzungsempfehlungen_Industrie4_0.pdf. Accessed Apr 2018
14. Lüder, A., Pauly, J., Rosendahl, R., Biffl, S., Rinker, F.: Support for engineering chain migration towards multi-disciplinary engineering chains. In: 14th IEEE International Conference on Automation Science and Engineering (CASE 2018), Proceedings, Munich, Germany (2018)
15. Winkler, D., Biffl, S., Steininger, H.: Integration von heterogenen Engineering Daten mit AutomationML und dem AML.hub: Konsistente Daten über Fachbereichs-grenzen hinweg, develop3 systems engineering, vol. 3 pp. 62–64 (2015)
16. Mordinyi, R., Winkler, D., Ekaputra, F.J., Wimmer, M., Biffl, S.: Investigating model slicing capabilities on integrated plant models with AutomationML. In: 21th IEEE International Conference on Emerging Technologies and Factory Automation (ETFA 2016), Proceedings-CD, Berlin, Germany, September 2016
17. Winkler, D., Wimmer, M., Berardinelli, L., Biffl, S.: Towards model quality assurance for multi-disciplinary engineering. In: Biffl, S., Lüder, A., Gerhard, D. (eds.) Multi-Disciplinary Engineering for Cyber-Physical Production Systems, pp. 433–457. Springer, Cham (2017). https://doi.org/10.1007/978-3-319-56345-9_16

Towards a Flexible and Secure Round-Trip-Engineering Process for Production Systems Engineering with Agile Practices

Dietmar Winkler[1,2(✉)], Felix Rinker[1,2], and Peter Kieseberg[3,4]

[1] Christian Doppler Laboratory for Security and Quality Improvement
in the Production System Lifecycle (CDL-SQI), Institute of Information Systems
Engineering, Information and Software Engineering Group,
TU Wien, Vienna, Austria
{dietmar.winkler, felix.rinker}@tuwien.ac.at
[2] Institute of Information Systems Engineering,
Information and Software Engineering Group, TU Wien, Vienna, Austria
[3] Secure Business Austria (SBA) Research, Vienna, Austria
PKieseberg@sba-research.org
[4] University of Applied Sciences, St. Pölten, Austria
peter.kieseberg@fhstp.ac.at

Abstract. In *Production Systems Engineering* (PSE), many projects conceptually follow the plan of traditional waterfall processes with sequential process steps and limited security activities, while engineers actually work in parallel and distributed groups following a *Round-Trip-Engineering* (RTE) process. Unfortunately, the applied RTE process in PSE is coarse-grained, i.e., often data are exchanged via E-Mail and integrated seldom and inefficiently as the RTE process is not well supported by methods and tools that facilitate efficient and secure data exchange. Thus, there is a need for frequent synchronization in a secure way to enable engineers building on a stable and baseline of engineering data. We build on Scrum, as an established agile engineering process, and security best practices to support flexible and secure RTE processes. In this paper, we introduce and initially evaluate an efficient and secure RTE process for PSE, augmented with agile practices, and discuss the identification and mitigation of security concerns and risks. First results show that the augmented RTE process can provide strong benefits from agile practices for the collaboration of engineers in PSE environments. Security practices can be added but need to be balanced well regarding sufficient mitigation of security risks and extra effort for engineers to ensure an overall benefit to both engineers and the management.

Keywords: Production Systems Engineering · Agile practices
Round-Trip Engineering · Security

D. Winkler et al. (Eds.): SWQD 2019, LNBIP 338, pp. 14–30, 2019.
https://doi.org/10.1007/978-3-030-05767-1_2

1 Introduction

In *Production Systems Engineering* (PSE) projects, various disciplines, such as plant planning, mechanical and electrical engineers as well as process automation and simulation engineers, collaborate in a common project, such as in development projects for manufacturing plants [6] or steel mills [2]. Work groups in these disciplines act as business centers that exchange data to develop and validate engineering plans. The official process often is pictured as a traditional sequential waterfall process [22] with limited security practices. However, engineers typically work in parallel in local groups following an incremental *Round-Trip-Engineering* (RTE) process [11]. In the RTE process, engineers from different disciplines take turns to develop engineering plans for a scope of work, not necessarily in a pre-defined sequence but as contributions from individual work groups. Because of parallel and distributed working teams and need for a stable baseline of engineering artifacts within a project, there is a need for a strong support for (a) flexible data exchange mechanism and (b) security considerations for data exchange to overcome limitations of unsecure communication and data exchange.

Typically, the RTE process in PSE is coarse-grained, i.e., engineering data are often exchanged infrequently with large amount of data point instead of continuous and frequent data synchronization of small data pieces. In industry practice, spreadsheets are often used as data containers and transferred via E-Mail. However, coarse-grained approaches lead to the risk of inconsistent (and often outdated) data bases and high manual rework effort. Unfortunately, data exchange is not well supported by methods and tools that facilitate efficient and secure data exchange. In context of security, engineers often apply security practices available within the organization (e.g., user access control). However, data security is often not well supported and there is no support if data changes are allowed at a defined point in time within the project course, e.g., after customer release of a defined set of data. Thus, there is also the need for better security support for data changes along the project course.

Main stakeholders in PSE projects include individual engineers, project managers, and business managers [3]. *Engineers* in different disciplines aim for effective and efficient collaboration as consumers and producers of data from and for other engineers in the organization and external partners. *Project managers* aim at fast and efficient engineering plan development. Further, *business managers* want better overview on the actual engineering project status between project milestones to focus on the mitigation of considerable risks from rework in the engineering process. Recently, security awareness has increased making traceability of data changes a priority to address security risks, such as malicious changes to engineering data and engineering knowledge theft [10, 17].

Based on the need for efficient and secure data exchange and for deriving an overview on the project progress, a set of challenges arises in PSE: Most challenges come from the *risky informal backflow of engineering changes* coming from later engineering stages back to earlier stages due to changes of requirements or of design aspects. This informal backflow can lead to an insufficient overview on open and completed tasks between engineering groups, such as the tracking of change propagation. Additional risk comes from *unauthorized access to engineering data*, e.g., from an organizational perspective where some engineers may not even see a defined (sub) set of engineering data or from project perspective where engineers are allowed to change engineering artifacts per se but may not be allowed to not change data without specific permission after a milestone has passed, e.g., after customer release. While *security risks* are known to be important, these risks are often not sufficiently visible and hard to address. In particular, the extra effort and cost for improving security raises conflicts with making the engineering process more efficient, where efficiency has in many cases higher priority. In addition, security risks often arise due to a combination of different technologies or interfaces without proper security engineering, thus security is a multi-stage issue in PSE. To address collaboration, data interoperability, quality and security issues, criteria for a good solution include (a) efficient engineering at low extra cost for flexible collaboration and for security practices; (b) good overview on the actual status of work for engineers in distributed work groups and for project management; and (c) effective mitigation of relevant risks in the RTE process.

A truly sequential engineering in a waterfall process [14] approach is in many cases not a viable process option due to overly long project duration and dependability between the sequential phases. The traditional and more flexible RTE process [11] is widely used but, surprisingly, not well supported. In contrast, business informatics has successfully used agile software engineering practices in the last 15 years, supported by methods, tools, and a range of security approaches [1].

Main goal of this paper focuses on integrating agile and security best practices in a RTE process to enable flexible (agile), efficient, and secure data exchange in PSE projects.

Therefore, in this paper, we introduce the innovative engineering method of an extended RTE process in PSE augmented with agile practices and security practices. Agile practices aim at supporting flexible and frequent data synchronization steps. First, we will identify requirements for flexibility and security for the RTE process in PSE. Then, we will conceptually evaluate the RTE process against these requirements in the following variants: (a) the traditional RTE process; (b) the RTE process augmented with agile practices; and (c) the RTE process augmented both with agile and with secure practices. First results of a conceptual evaluation show that the RTE process augmented with agile practices has promising benefits for the collaboration of engineers with frequent changes of PSE artefacts.

The remainder of this paper is structured as follows: Sect. 2 summarizes related work on *Production Systems Engineering* (PSE), Agile Software Development, and Security in PSE processes. Section 3 introduces to the Research Issues and Sect. 4 an illustrating use case. We present the RTE process with agile practices in Sect. 5 and a conceptual evaluation in Sect. 6. Finally, Sect. 7 discusses the results, concludes and identifies future work.

2   Related Work

This section summarizes related work on *Production Systems Engineering*, *Agile Software Development*, and *Security* in PSE processes as foundation for improving the RTE process.

2.1   Production Systems Engineering

In *Production Systems Engineering (PSE)* the collaboration of engineers coming from different disciplines is success critical for engineering projects [26]. In industry practice the plan typically follows a sequential (and waterfall-like) process approach [14]. However, in practice, individual engineers work in parallel and distributed teams. Thus, there is a strong need for efficient and effective data exchange to build on a stable engineering baseline in all phases of the engineering project. Figure 1 presents such a sequential engineering process with parallel engineering activities and integrated Quality Assurance (QA) activities. Another need arises from changes that come from later engineering phases and that can have a major impact on product quality and the project progress. Thus, the collaboration of engineers in a heterogeneous and multi-disciplinary project environment strongly depends on efficient and sufficiently secure data exchange mechanisms to provide a stable foundation for project work.

Therefore, appropriate tool support is needed [3]. In industry practice a set of various approaches aim at addressing PSE engineering needs:

- *All-in-one* solutions cover all related disciplines within a common engineering environment which would work well within an established project scope. All-in-one solutions typically include a vendor dependability of all related project stakeholders which might make it difficult in project consortia, where various engineering organizations (with different tool settings) should collaborate. Furthermore, this type of solutions typically focus on most important features (relevant for many different organizations) leaving specific needs of individual disciplines out of scope. In engineering practice, engineers often apply different specific tools often with non-standardized data interchange formats that require comprehensive data trans-formations for exchanging engineering data.
- *Point-to-point* solutions aim at overcoming these interoperability requirements by providing direct connection between two or more related specialized tools for data exchange purposes. In practice, individual data exchange mechanisms between pairs of communicating tools have been implemented with a focus on a specific project and/or organization and suffer from strong limitations on maintainability and extensibility. Tool or data format changes, caused by updates have to be considered accordingly.
- *Integration platforms* [13, 25] typically provide a common data source and defined data interfaces that connect individual tools to the common data source. However, engineers have to (a) negotiate common data concepts for linking various disci-plines once at the beginning of the project and (b) provide tool support for efficient and secure data exchange. Note that often these common concepts (and tool solutions) are reusable for similar project settings.

A common and/or agreed data set and corresponding data formats are pre-conditions for efficient data exchange to minimize transformation activities. For sup-porting the harmonization of related tool data as enabler for efficient data exchange, *AutomationML* [4], a standardized data exchange format, can be used. However, tool support is needed to provide the required functionality for efficient and sufficiently

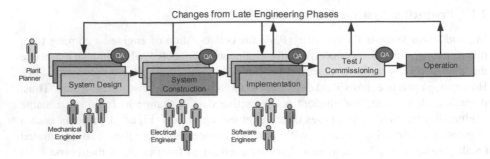

Fig. 1. Sequential engineering process with parallel engineering activities.

secure data exchange. While security risks are known to be important, they are often not sufficiently visible and hard to address without extra effort and cost.

In the PSE context, engineers contribute in a pre-defined sequence of work as depicted in Fig. 1. However, in practice, engineers work in parallel in local groups or business centers following an incremental *Round-Trip-Engineering* (RTE) *process* where data gets exchanged between two parties via e-mail or data storage systems with only limited interoperability and security capabilities.

Figure 2 depicts a traditional RTE process approach involving the plant planning discipline and three engineering disciplines, i.e., mechanical, electrical, and software. Engineers use individual and local data models for development and share a subset of needed data with directly related disciplines. Note that the traditional RTE process does not include any data exchange mechanisms but focuses on data exchange via proprietary data formats and a data exchange via E-Mail. Basically, individual transformations (such as provided by a point-to-point integration strategy) is needed. To overcome data format deviations, *AutomationML* can be used in the RTE process. The plant planner provides the general plant topology, e.g., using the *AutomationML* description language. Individual engineering disciplines contribute to the common project using specific tools and data models to exchange their engineering data. Although engineers work in parallel and contribute to the common work result from their discipline specific view, there is only limited flexibility and communication to accommodate for frequent changes (common in parallel engineering).

Our previous work include a prototype implementation of a RTE process in a PSE context on a tool level[1] without considering flexible (agile) engineering practices or security concerns. However, an integration platform is used for providing mechanisms for a more flexible and efficient data exchange [26]. However, this prototype solution does not support flexible (agile) practices or security. Agile concepts that have been successfully used in *Business Informatics* could help to overcome some of these limitations with focus on flexibility. In addition, security awareness has increased [23] making traceability of data changes a priority to address security risks, such as malicious changes to engineering data or engineering knowledge theft.

---

[1] See the basic RTE Use Case: http://qse.ifs.tuwien.ac.at/wp-content/uploads/1703_EN.pdf.

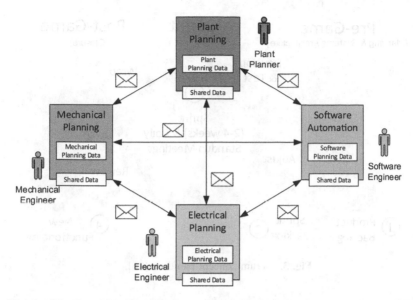

Fig. 2. "Coarse-grained" round-trip engineering with e-mail based data exchange.

2.2 Agile Software Development

In *Software Engineering*, the need for more flexible software engineering processes has been addressed since the early 2000s. Based on the *Agile Manifesto*[2] a goal (among others) was to support frequent changes in software engineering artifacts and to improve communication and coordination in the software engineering team. *Scrum* [16] is a well-established software engineering approach, frequently used in academia and industry.

Main goal of *Scrum* is to deliver integrated executable software versions frequently and efficiently. Figure 3 depicts the basic *Scrum* process organized in three main phases, i.e., *(1) Pre-Game, (2) Sprint*, and *(3) Post-Game*, to deliver new functionality *(4)* of software. The *Pre-Game* phase defines the basic software architecture, a *Product Backlog* (Fig. 3, step 1) holds a prioritized set of requirements or features, which may change over time. Changes could come from customer input or from changes derived from prior development phases or tests. At the beginning of a *Sprint*, the engineering team transfers a manageable pile of features into the *Sprint Backlog* (Fig. 3, step 2). A team of engineers has to complete all features in the *Sprint Backlog* within 2 to 4 weeks, a typical *Sprint* duration (Fig. 3, step 3). In a *Sprint* there are short daily standup meetings for progress reporting and for problem solving. At the end of a successful *Sprint*, a new version of running software has to be available (Fig. 3, step 4). In *Software Engineering*, this process is supported by tools, e.g., *Jira*[3], for issue assignment and tracking, to manage the backlogs and tasks.

---

[2] Agile Manifest: http://agilemanifesto.org/.

[3] Atlassian Jira: https://www.atlassian.com/software/jira.

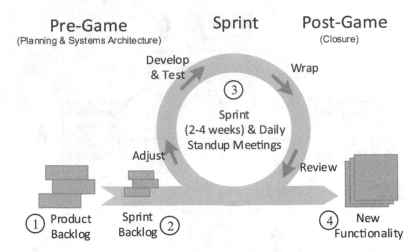

Fig. 3. Scrum concept based on [16].

In PSE, engineers typically follow a coarse-grained parallel engineering process (see Fig. 2), embedded within a sequential overall project process. Based on experiences in *Software Engineering*, the concept of *Scrum* could be a promising approach in PSE to support (frequent) engineering plan changes and to improve the communication within or between the engineering teams. However, adaptations of the process and tool appropriate support are needed to address needs of the PSE community.

2.3   Security in Production Systems Engineering

In recent years, security awareness has increased making the traceability of data changes a priority to address security risks, such as malicious changes to engineering data or engineering knowledge theft [23]. There are several typical Security threats from *Business Informatics* that are also relevant in PSE with focus on cyber-physical production systems.

Communication security. During the development phase, communication with stakeholders and between experts is of vital importance. Communication, especially with external partners, is the Achilles heel with respect to security, as ill-defined interfaces allow for a multitude of attacks with different targets. Within a PSE, industrial espionage is an important security risk, as is the manipulation of assets in order to introduce obstacles to the production process, or even corrupt the result of production. Securing communication requires considerable changes to the traditional PSE process, especially introducing clearly defined communication interfaces and paths, but also integrating security measures like encryption into specialized engineering tools [18].

Data security. Knowledge and data are two examples of the vital assets of any designer of production systems, thus industrial espionage is one of the most important security threats. In addition to ex-ante strategies for securing vital information, ex-post techniques need to be considered. While these, contrary to ex-ante strategies like secure knowledge repositories, do not actually thwart the extraction of vital business information, ex-post security techniques allow for the detection of leaked content when it is encountered. Important techniques include watermarking and fingerprinting of data and other information in order to enable a proof of ownership, or even a proof of which party leaked the data (attack attribution) [15].

Process-related security is an additional issue for the PSE process because of changing security-related aspects throughout backflows. Since security depends on nearly every aspect of a system that involves communication, even slight, often nonfunctional, changes can lead to serious deterioration of the security level. For example, changing a chip-set to another version might introduce an unprotected wireless communication interface, which must be taken into account for security analysis. Furthermore, security measures might also introduce issues into the overall design. For example, intrusion detection systems typically alter system performance, which might be undesirable or even require the installation of other technological solutions. Thus, security mechanisms need to be taken account in every step of the PSE process, especially when producing software. The *Secure Software Development Lifecycle (SSDLC)* which introduces security at every step of the software development process [8]. In order to adopt such a process, a clear-cut agile development process sporting well-defined hand-over points and communication channels is required.

Trusted Computing. One major issue in integrated platforms lies in providing trust, e.g., for authentication. In 2000 the "Trusted Computing Platform Alliance" provided a whitepaper [19] motivating and finally introduced so-called "Trusted Platform Modules" [20], a distinct, separate component in a computing platform that provides a set of functions independent from the rest of the platform to enable so-called "roots of trust", like aggregation of measurements, storage of data and trusted reporting of results. Still, even modern paradigms of this kind like Intel's TXT technology [7] have been targeted by attacks like Foreshadow [21], even though these technologies are designed to withstand attacks for a very long time. Since providing trust (e.g., by securely handling private keys) is essential for many widely adopted security architectures and changes in these trusted computing appliances are hard to impossible, this poses an important problem when considering the adoption of standard security strategies for machines and appliances with a long life-span.

3   Research Issues and Approach

Based on related work and discussions with industry partners, we have identified a set of research issues to include flexibility and sufficient security in PSE processes, especially in the RTE process approach.

RI.1.   How can **agile practices** from Business Informatics support a RTE process in
        Production Systems Engineering? Agile principles such as flexibility, ticket
        assignment, issue tracking and tracing, project overview for business and
        project management, and frequent iterations for a selected system scope, are

promising to improve traditional PSE processes. The question is, how these approaches from business informatics can be applied to PSE and RTE processes. Based on a scrum-based approach, derived from *Software Engineering* in *Business Informatics*, we apply this approach to individual disciplines in the PSE context.

RI.2.   *How can **security practices** from Business Informatics support a RTE process in Production Systems Engineering?* Communication data, and process security concerns have gained importance in the past years, with the advancement of internet applications to PSE and to production systems. However, new security practices, e.g., based on the SSDLC, in a process often require risk mitigation and extra effort and cost for implementation. Thus, there will be a trade-off between making PSE processes more effective and efficient on the one hand side and sufficiently secure on the other hand side. Thus, the main question is, how security practices can help to make PSE processes more secure, while mitigating the impact on reduced process efficiency and usability.

4   Illustrating Use Case and Requirements

This section introduces to an illustrating use case and summarize important requirements for RTE with agile and secure practices. We derived the requirements from related work and from discussions with industry partners in the PSE context.

4.1   Illustrating Use Case "Welding Cell"

A welding cell is an important component within an automotive manufacturing process [12]. In PSE projects, engineers develop parts of a production system in distinct and sequential steps. In this context, the scope of an iterative development step/sprint is a production system part, such as a welding cell or a set of machines in a work cell. Engineers develop details of the engineering plan in several steps, e.g., a first level of detail may be to select the relevant devices for a work cell, a second level may concern the network to link these devices, a later level of detail the automation or simulation of a device or of a set of collaborating devices. Therefore, candidates for iterative development steps/sprints can be (a) to develop system parts in detail, e.g., one welding cell after the other or (b) following a top down approach, i.e., starting with the overall production system plan, then include more detailed plans iteratively. This iterative way of working allows engineers to work incrementally and share partial work early among the disciplines to facilitate working in parallel and validating rough plans before investing into detail planning. However, incremental collaboration can only be efficient and robust if supported with appropriate methods and tools that allow defining back-flows in engineering and support the impact analysis of changes in one engineering discipline on other disciplines to efficiently propagate change needs and task in the overall engineering team. Unfortunately, most engineering tools are well designed for developing engineering plans for a specific discipline only, but are not designed to interact with other disciplines or overall project management making it hard to analyze the impact of local changes within an incremental and iterative development process.

4.2 Data Management and Security Requirements for PSE

Based on the generic use (Sect. 4.1) and observations and discussions with industry partners in context of PSE projects, we collected and analyzed basic requirements for improving the RTE process approach to address flexibility and security issues. Note that the summarized requirements represent selected key requirements that need to be addressed by an agile and secure RTE process. Table 1 presents the selected set of derived requirements. Note that RE-1-x cover requirements with focus on collaboration and data exchange and RE-2x takes into account security concerns that need to be addressed.

Table 1. Requirements for flexible and secure RTE processes.

ID	Requirement and Capabilities
RE-1-1	*Support for effective and efficient Change Management.* Efficiently propagating engineering changes to related disciplines
RE-1-2	*Traceability.* Visibility of data flows (and backflows) between work groups as foundation for analyzing expected and actual data flows
RE-1-3	*Project Monitoring.* Project status analysis of engineering data regarding maturity and validation of data elements
RE-2-1	*Communication Security*, i.e., secure communication between disciplines via a common data exchange platform
RE-2-2	*Data security*, i.e., controlled access to defined engineering data, depending on individual views
RE-2-3	*Process-related Security* in case of changes and engineering backflows or access after a reaching defined milestone

5 Proposed RTE Process with Agile and with Secure Practices

Based on agile practices, derived from *Software Engineering* and *Business Informatics*, and secure practices, derived from *Business Informatics* and *Software Security*, we propose an adapted/extended RTE process for PSE with agile and secure practices. The augmented agile and secure RTE process is to facilitate (a) efficient, effective, and controlled data exchange via a common data exchange platform (following the *Integration Platform* approach) and (b) secure data exchange with focus on data, communication, and process security.

Figure 4 presents the proposed PSE process approach with agile and secure practices:

- A centralized *Data Exchange Platform* holds common project data that is used for discipline specific engineering activities. Engineers work in their local views and

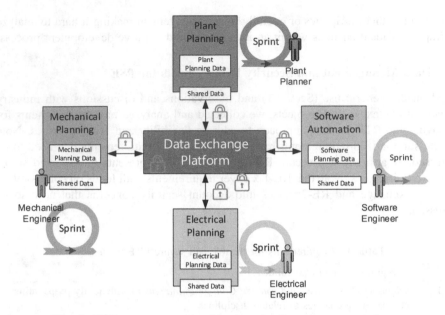

Fig. 4. RTE process concept with adapted agile and secure practices

exchange relevant data via defined data interfaces to the data exchange platform bi-
directionally (*shared data* in individual disciplines). Note that we used *AutomationML* [5] as a common data format for data exchange purposes.

- The *Plant planner* provides the basic structure of the plant in *AutomationML* as a
  hierarchical structure of the planned plant. We consider this step as part of the *Pre-
  Game* in the *Scrum* terminology.
- *Individual disciplines*, such as mechanical, electrical and software engineers,
  develop local plans in a flexible and agile way following the *Scrum* process [16]
  with selected agile practices [9]: *Feature Backlogs* hold overall project goals and
  sets of requirements *(User Stories)* for the overall project and current sprints. *Jira* is
  used for task assignment and issue tracking. Furthermore, Jira facilitates versioning
  and change tracking. Reported and tracked issues represent enablers for project
  planning and monitoring by using *Burndown Charts*. Furthermore, *Scrum Boards*,
  available via Jira, provides a comprehensive overview on the current project status,
  relevant for project managers and business people. However, for exchanging data
  between individual disciplines and the data exchange platform, transformers and
  converters are needed to map individual data from one view to the other, e.g., by
  addressing different semantic meanings or value ranges in different views.
- Beyond agile practices, *security measures*, such as encryption (secure data
  exchange between disciplines and the data exchange platform), watermarking or
  fingerprinting (authenticity, data integrity, and correctness) can address communication and data security aspects. Data access rights, data status, and communication
  processes, implemented in Jira support process security aspects. Exchanging
  engineering data via a central exchange platform supports the implementation of

security mechanisms, such as authentication, access control or process control mechanisms between internal and external project partners.

6 Conceptual Evaluation

We present an application use case of the adapted/extended RTE process and a conceptual evaluation of the proposed process approach.

6.1 Application Use Case: Round-Trip-Engineering (RTE)

Round-Trip Engineering (RTE) is an often-used process in PSE requiring parallel planning, support for tracing changes and engineering tool data integration in a common data repository. The illustrative use case, introduced in Sect. 4.1 is an example for a PSE process, observed at our industry partner. Based on the initial requirements, defined in Sect. 4.2 we designed an adapted/extended RTE process.

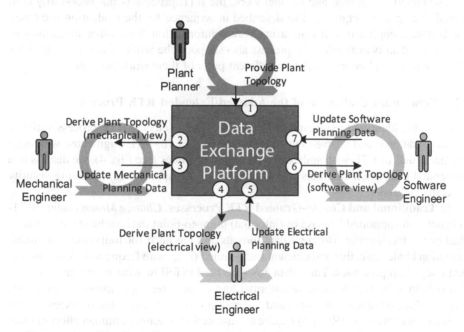

Fig. 5. Agile round-trip-engineering process approach.

Figure 5 presents an application of a RTE process with agile practices consisting of seven application steps:

(1) The *Plant Planner* commits the general plant topology by using *AutomationML* to the integrated engineering platform.
(2) *Mechanical Engineers* retrieve the mechanical view of the current plant topology, add mechanical planning data and engineering artifacts in the local view.

(3) After completing the work in the mechanical local view, the *Mechanical Engineer* commits updated planning data and related engineering artifacts, such as documents, to the data exchange platform.
(4) *Electrical Engineers* check out the electrical view of the latest planning data, add electrical planning data respective related engineering artifacts to the electrical view.
(5) Electrical changes are committed back to the data exchange platform by the *Electrical Engineer*.
(6) The *Software Engineer* checks out the software view of the current planning data. He updates the view with the software planning data respective related engineering artifacts.
(7) Finally, the *Software Engineer* commits software changes back to the data exchange platform.

Note that *Engineering Artifacts* can be documents containing data sheets, mechanical or electrical drawings, program code, or 3D representations of components. These documents are available as PDFs via external links in the common data repository (if needed by the individual views).

To support distributed and parallel work, the RTE process is not necessarily conducted in a specific sequence (just described in sequence for the evaluation use case). For instance, engineers can start using partial information from other disciplines as soon as the data is available. The process also supports the work of multiple engineers of the same discipline in parallel on different parts of their work package.

6.2 Conceptual Evaluation of the Adapted/Extended RTE Process

Based on the identified requirements (see Table 1) and selected RTE process variants, i.e., (a) traditional and coarse-grained RTE (see Fig. 2), (b) RTE augmented with agile practices, and (c) RTE with agile and with secure practices (see Fig. 4), we discuss in a conceptual evaluation strengths and limitations of the approaches, including security concerns and risks.

In **Traditional and Coarse-Grained RTE Processes**, *Change Management* (RE-1-1) is not well supported because of (informal) point-to-point data exchange, e.g., via E-Mail or via file transfer. Different data formats and the need for individual data transformation hinder effective and efficient fine-grained (i.e., more frequent or "continuous" data integration processes. Thus, data flows are hard to follow with strong limitations to *Traceability* (RE-1-2) because of informal and often insecure communication paths. *Project Monitoring* and consistent and accurate project views and the overview on the overall project progress (RE-1-3) require a considerable amount of human effort in time-consuming and error-prone data collection, aggregation, and updating activities. Thus, tasks for getting an overall project overview are executed on request and not on a regular basis which hinders effective and efficient project monitoring and control.

With focus on security concerns, informal communication and data paths often hinder *Process-Related Security* (RE-2-3) because of strong limitations on the availability of information and communication flows. *Communication Security* (RE-2-1) and *Data Security* (RE-2-2), e.g., encrypting, typically depend on the development environments and implemented security measures, but often depend on the IT strategy of the organization. Authenticity, data integrity, and correctness of engineering data strongly relies on the project participants and could not be supported sufficiently.

PSE Augmented with Agile Practices from Business Informatics. A common data exchange platform augmented with agile practices (Sect. 5) overcomes some of the limitations of the traditional RTE process. Frequent and efficient data exchange supports *Change Management* (RE-1-1), e.g., via ticketing and versioning. Integrated tool support for individual process steps/sprints enables *Traceability* (RE-1-2) and facilitates effective and efficient Project *Monitoring* (RE-1-3), e.g., by analyzing tickets or artifact versions, or via *Scrum Boards* or *Burndown Charts*. Shifting data exchange from point-to-point data exchange between related disciplines to the data exchange via a common platform, allows centralizing access control (*Communication Security*, RE-2-1), and increases data security with a focus on integrated data models that are available in the data exchange platform (*Data Security*, RE-2-2). Finally, workflows implemented in the data exchange platform allow controlling *Process-Related Security* (RE-2-3).

PSE with Agile and with Secure Practices from Business Informatics. As discussed in the previous subsection the adapted RTE process with agile practices significantly improves *Change Management* (RE-1-1), *Traceability* of data and data changes (RE-1–2), and enables an overview on the overall project progress and, thus, supports *Project Monitoring* (RE-1–3). Furthermore, security measures can be introduced based on a clearly defined RTE process with tool support. For instance, to address *Communication Security* (RE-2-1), encryption can be used on the engineering tool side as well on the platform side. To protect intellectual property and to address *Data Security* (RE-2–2), concepts of watermarking or fingerprinting can be applied on top of communication security mechanisms. Finally, *Process-Related Security* (RE-2-3) can be addressed by improved communication mechanisms (embedded within engineering workflow on the data exchange platform) and enriched with security mechanisms.

Although security practices can be added quite easily, these practices need to be balanced well regarding sufficient mitigation of security risks and extra effort for engineers to ensure an overall benefit both to engineers and to management.

7 Discussion, Conclusion, and Future Work

While the (traditional) *Round-Trip-Engineering* (RTE) process in *Production Systems Engineering* (PSE) is widely used, unfortunately, this process is not well supported by methods and tools that facilitate efficient, frequent and fine-grained and secure data exchange as foundation for project monitoring and control.

In this paper, we introduced and conceptually evaluated as an innovative engineering method an adapted/extended RTE process in PSE augmented (a) with agile practices and (b) with security practices that have been successfully used in Business Informatics over the past decades. Based on requirements for efficient and secure data exchange mechanisms in PSE, we focused on two Research Questions: (RQ1) how *agile practices* and (RQ2) how *security practices*, derived from *Business Informatics*, can support the RTE in Production Systems Engineering Processes.

Table 2. Conceptual evaluation: traditional, agile, and agile & secure RTE processes (++ well supported, + supported, o neutral support, - weak support, – no support).

Requirements and capabilities	RTE process variants		
	Traditional RTE	RTE with agile practices	RTE with agile and secure practices
RE-1-1: Change Management	-	++	++
RE-1-2: Traceability	–	++	++
RE-1-3: Project Monitoring	-	++	++
RE-2-1: Communication Sec.	o	o	++
RE-2-2: Data Security	-	o	++
RE-2-3: Process Security	–	+	++

Basic requirements focus on the need for efficient *Change Management* and *Traceability* of engineering data across involved disciplines [24]. Often data exchange is executed in an informal way, e.g., data exchange via E-Mail with limited tool support for merging data coming from different sources. Thus, high manual effort is required to keep an overview on the overall project status for *Project Monitoring*. With focus on security, concepts strongly rely on the capabilities of the IT infrastructure applied within the project and the organization. However, *Communication, Data,* and *Process Security* are critical in context of intellectual properties and data exchange. Table 2 summarizes identified requirements in context of (a) *traditional RTE processes*, (b) *RTE with agile practices*, and (c) *RTE with agile and secure practices* from *Business Informatics*.

In traditional (coarse-grained) RTE processes (see Fig. 2), data exchange is often based on manual and human activities with significant effort and cost at the data consumer side. Without explicit security mechanisms, the security level in practice depends on the basic IT strategy of the organization. For agile RTE processes, data exchange can be based on a central data exchange platform with an adjustable set of security considerations, e.g., for authentication. Process security in terms of workflow control can be configured as an integral part of the platform. Finally, RTE processes with agile and secure practices provide the benefits of agile RTE and selected security concepts, such as encryption, watermarking or fingerprinting.

Based on a first conceptual evaluation and discussions with industry partners, we can conclude that the augmented RTE process can provide considerable benefits from agile practices for the collaboration of engineers and the management. Security aspects rely on the IT security strategy of the organization (e.g., with focus on the development environment) but can be added within the adapted/extended RTE process. However, the integration of security practices need to be balanced well regarding sufficient mitigation of security risks and extra effort for engineers to ensure an overall benefit to both engineers and management.

Future work will focus on a set of different research directions: (a) Elicit in more detail key requirements for the agile and secure application of the RTE process to improve the current conceptual prototype; (b) Investigate how to ensure the usability of promising security practices for PSE participants to mitigate the risk of undermining security by circumventing the agreed practices in favor for more efficient but unsecure work practices; and (c) Evaluate current prototypes in a series of case studies in a real world setting.

Acknowledgment. The financial support by the Austrian Federal Ministry for Digital, Business and Enterprise and the National Foundation for Research, Technology and Development is gratefully acknowledged.

References

1. Abrahamsson, P., Salo, O., Ronkainen J., Warsta J.: Agile Software Development Methods: Review and Analysis. VTT Publication 478 (2002)
2. Biffl, S., Lüder, A., Gerhard, D. (eds.): Multi-Disciplinary Engineering for Cyber-Physical Production Systems. Springer, Heidelberg (2017). https://doi.org/10.1007/978-3-319-56345-9
3. Biffl, S., Lüder, A., Winkler, D.: Multi-disciplinary engineering for Industrie 4.0: semantic challenges and needs (Chap. 2). In: Biffl, S., Sabou, M. (eds.) Semantic Web Technologies for Intelligent Engineering Applications, pp. 17–51. Springer, Heidelberg (2016). https://doi.org/10.1007/978-3-319-41490-4_2
4. Drath, R., Lüder, A., Peschke, J., Hundt, L.: AutomationML - the glue for seamless automation engineering. In: Proceedings of the IEEE International Conference on Emerging Technologies and Factory Automation (ETFA), pp. 616–623 (2008)
5. Drath, R. (ed.): Datenaustausch in der Anlagenplanung mit AutomationML Integration von CAEX, PLCopen XML und COLLADA. Springer, Heidelberg (2010). https://doi.org/10.1007/978-3-642-04674-2
6. ElMaraghy, H.A. (ed.): Changeable and Reconfigurable Manufacturing Systems. Springer, London (2009). https://doi.org/10.1007/978-1-84882-067-8
7. Grawrock, G.: Dynamics of a Trusted Platform: A Building Block Approach. Intel Press, Santa Clara (2009)
8. Howard, M., Lipner, S.: The Security Development Lifecycle, vol. 8. Microsoft Press, Redmond (2006)
9. Leffingwell, D.: Scaling Software Agility: Best Practices for Large Enterprises. Pearson Education, London (2007)
10. Lee, E.A.: Cyber physical systems: design challenges. In: Proceedings of the 11th IEEE International Symposium on Object Oriented Real-Time Distributed Computing (ISORC), pp. 363–369. IEEE (20080
11. Medvidovic, N., Egyed, A., Rosenblum, D.S.: Round-trip software engineering using UML: from architecture to design and back. In: Proceedings of the 2nd International Workshop on Object-Oriented Reengineering (WOOR), pp. 1–8 (1999)
12. Michalos, G., Makris, S., Papakostas, P., Mourtzis, D., Chryssolouris, G.: Automotive assembly technologies review: challenges and outlook for a flexible and adaptive approach. J. Manuf. Sci. Technol. **2**, 81–91 (2010)
13. Moser, T., Biffl, S.: Semantic tool interoperability for engineering manufacturing systems. In: Proceedings of the 15th IEEE International Conference on Emerging Technologies and Factory Automation (ETFA) (2010)

14. Petersen, K., Wohlin, C., Baca, D.: The waterfall model in large-scale development. In: Bomarius, F., Oivo, M., Jaring, P., Abrahamsson, P. (eds.) PROFES 2009. LNBIP, vol. 32, pp. 386–400. Springer, Heidelberg (2009). https://doi.org/10.1007/978-3-642-02152-7_29
15. Pfleeger, C.P., Pfleeger, S.L.: Security in computing. In: Prentice Hall Professional Technical Reference (2002)
16. Schwaber, K., Beedle, M.: Agile Software Development with Scrum, vol. 1. Prentice Hall, Upper Saddle River (2002)
17. Shameli-Sendi, A., Aghababaei-Barzegar, R., Cheriet, M.: Taxonomy of information security risk assessment (ISRA). Comput. Secur. **57**, 14–30 (2016)
18. Slijepcevic, S., Potkonjak, M., Tsiatsis, V., Zimbeck, S., Srivastava, M.B.: On communication security in wireless ad-hoc sensor networks. In: Proceedings of the 11th IEEE Workshop on Enabling Technologies: Infrastructure for Collaborative Enterprises (WET ICE), pp. 139–144 (2002)
19. Trusted Computing Platform Alliance; Building A Foundation of Trust in the PC; Whitepaper (2000)
20. Trusted Computing Platform Alliance; Main Specification 1.1b; Trusted Computing Group 2003
21. Van Bulck, J., Piessens, F., Strackx, R.: Foreshadow: extracting the keys to the intel SGX kingdom with transient out-of-order execution. In: 27th USENIX Security Symposium. USENIX Association (2018)
22. Vyatkin, V.: Software engineering in industrial automation: state-of-the-art review. IEEE Trans. Ind. Inform. **9**(3), 1234–1249 (2013)
23. VDI: IT-security for industrial automation – general model. VDI guideline. VDI/VDE 2182 (2011)
24. Winkler, D., Moser, T., Mordinyi, R., Sunindyo, W., Biffl, S.: Engineering object change management process observation in distributed automation systems projects. In: Proceedings of 18th European System & Software Process Improvement and Innovation (EuroSPI), Industrial Track, pp. 8.25–8.36 (2011)
25. Winkler, D., Ekaputra, F., Biffl, S.: AutomationML review support in multi-disciplinary engineering environments. In: Proceedings of the 21st International Conference on Emerging Technologies and Factory Automation (ETFA). IEEE (2016)
26. Winkler, D., Sabou, M., Biffl, S.: Improving quality assurance in multi-disciplinary engineering environments with semantic technologies (Chap. 8). In: Kounis, L.D. (ed.) Quality Control and Assurance – An Ancient Greek Term ReMastered, pp. 177–200. INTEC Publishing, London (2017)

Software Quality and Process Improvement

Relating Verification and Validation Methods to Software Product Quality Characteristics: Results of an Expert Survey

Isela Mendoza[1], Marcos Kalinowski[2(✉)], Uéverton Souza[1],
and Michael Felderer[3]

[1] Fluminense Federal University, Niteroi, Brazil
{imendoza,ueverton}@ic.uff.br
[2] Pontifical Catholic University of Rio de Janeiro, Rio de Janeiro, Brazil
kalinowski@inf.puc-rio.br
[3] University of Innsbruck, Innsbruck, Austria
michael.felderer@uibk.ac.at

Abstract. **[Context]** Employing appropriate verification and validation (V&V) methods is essential to improve software product quality. However, while several V&V methods have been documented, little is known about how these methods relate to specific product quality characteristics. **[Goal]** The goal of this paper is to provide an initial configuration on the suitability of selected V&V methods to address ISO 25010 software product quality characteristics. **[Method]** Therefore, we compiled a list of V&V methods and conducted a survey with V&V experts, asking them to evaluate how well each V&V method allows for addressing the ISO 25010 characteristics. **[Results]** We received 19 answers from experts of 7 different countries. Our results express the aggregated expert opinion. It is noteworthy that the experts mostly agreed in their opinions, indicating consistency in the results. **[Conclusions]** This work provides the first result on the relationship between V&V methods and quality characteristics. We believe that the aggregated opinion of 19 experts can serve as a starting point for further investigations by other researchers and to provide an additional understanding to practitioners.

Keywords: Verification and validation methods · Software product quality

1 Introduction

Software quality can be defined as the degree to which a system meets the specified requirements and expectations of a customer or user [9]. For the industry, quality assurance in software development projects constitutes a high-cost activity. An adequate selection of verification and validation methods (V&V) to ensure that the product is correctly implemented and meets its specifications, is essential for reducing these costs [2, 4, 7].

Concerning software product quality, there are standards, such as ISO 25010 [5], specifying the product quality characteristics. V&V methods, on the other hand, are employed in order to assure software product quality. Unfortunately, the selection of

© Springer Nature Switzerland AG 2019
D. Winkler et al. (Eds.): SWQD 2019, LNBIP 338, pp. 33–44, 2019.
https://doi.org/10.1007/978-3-030-05767-1_3

different V&V methods as well as the interdependencies among them are still not well understood. Hence, the software industry faces the problem of choosing specific V&V methods to assure the quality of the software, since an inadequate selection of these methods may generate significant effort throughout the software development process and consequently high costs [2, 4, 7].

Taking into account the quality characteristics of the ISO 25010 standard [5], a series of V&V methods compiled mainly from the SWEBOK [1], and other sources [9, 10], the main goal of this work is to obtain an initial understanding on which V&V methods are the most appropriate ones to address each of the ISO 25010 characteristics, from the point of view of the software engineering experts. Therefore, we conducted a survey with a sample of 145 experts, all PhDs in software engineering, with relevant publications in the V&V area, and active in at least one of the following software engineering and V&V program committees: ICSE, ICST, ESEM, SEAA-SPPI, and SWQD.

In total, 19 experts from 7 different countries responded to the survey. The results provide an initial characterization of V&V methods against ISO 25010 quality characteristics. While our results still represent an initial understanding, the overall agreement among the experts reinforces our confidence that they represent a meaningful starting point for other researchers and that they can be used as an initial reference on the topic by the software industry. In response to one of the survey questions, experts also recommend new methods to be evaluated in future survey trials.

The paper is organized as follows. In Sect. 2, the background on the chosen V&V methods is presented. In Sect. 3, the ISO 25010 quality characteristics are described. In Sect. 4, the survey plan is outlined. In Sect. 5, we describe the survey operation, i.e., how the survey was conducted. In Sect. 6, the survey results are presented and analyzed. Finally, Sect. 7 contains the concluding remarks.

2 Software Verification and Validation Methods

Several V&V methods have been proposed throughout the years. Hereafter we detail a selection of such methods, representing an aggregated compilation of the methods presented in the SWEBOK [1] and two books focused respectively on software product quality and peer reviews [9, 10]. Table 1 shows the classification of the selected V&V methods and a very short description of each of them based on the descriptions provided in [1, 9, 10].

Table 1. Description and classification type of the selected V&V methods

Classification	Methods	Short description
Based on Intuition and Experience	Ad hoc Testing	Tests are derived relying on the software engineer's skill, intuition, and experience with similar programs
	Exploratory Testing	Is defined as simultaneous learning, test design, and test execution, that is, the tests are not defined in advance in an established test plan, are dynamically designed, executed, and modified
Input Domain-Based	Equivalence Partitioning	Involves partitioning the input domain into a collection of subsets (or equivalent classes) based on a pacified criterion or relation
	Pair wise Testing	Test cases are derived by combining interesting values for every pair of a set of input variables instead of considering all possible combinations
	Boundary-Value Analysis	Test cases are chosen on or near the boundaries of the input domain of variables, with the underlying rationale that many faults tend to concentrate near the extreme values of inputs
	Random Testing	Tests are generated purely at random. This form of testing falls under the heading of input domain testing since the input domain must be known to be able to pick random points within it
	Cause-Effect Graphing	Represent the logical relationships between conditions (roughly, inputs) and actions (roughly, outputs). Test cases are systematically derived by considering combinations of conditions and their corresponding resultant actions
Code-Based	Control Flow-Based Criteria	Are aimed to covering all the statements, blocks of statements, or specified combinations of statements in a program
	Data Flow-Based Criteria	In data flow-based testing, the control flow graph is annotated with information about how the program variables are defined, used, and killed (undefined)
Fault-Based	Error Guessing	In error guessing, test cases are specifically designed by software engineers who try to anticipate the most plausible faults in a given program
	Mutation Testing	A mutant is a slightly modified version of the program under test, differing from it by a small syntactic change
Usage-Based	Operational Profile	In testing for reliability evaluation (also called operational testing), the test environment reproduces the operational environment of the software, or the operational profile, as closely as possible. The goal is to infer from the observed test results the future reliability of the software when in actual use
	Usability Inspection Methods	Usability principles can provide guidelines for discovering problems in the design of the user interface. Are also called usability inspection methods, including: Heuristic evaluation or User Observation Heuristics, Heuristic estimation, Cognitive walkthrough, Pluralistic walkthrough, Feature inspection, Consistency inspection, Standards inspection and Formal usability inspection
Model-Based Testing	Finite-State Machines	By modeling a program as a finite state machine, tests can be selected in order to cover the states and transitions
	Workflow Models	Workflow models specify a sequence of activities performed by humans and/or software applications, usually represented through graphical notations

(continued)

Table 1. (*continued*)

Classification	Methods	Short description
Reviews	Walkthrough	The purpose of a systematic walk-through is to evaluate a software product. A walkthrough may be conducted for educating an audience regarding a software product
	Peer Review or Desk Checking	The authors do not explain the artifact. They give it to one or more colleagues who read it and give feedback. The aim is to find defects and get comments on the style
	Technical Review	Further formalizes the review process. They are often also management reviews or project status reviews with the aim to make decisions about the project progress. In general, a group discusses the artefacts and decides about the content
	Inspection	The purpose of an inspection is to detect and identify software product anomalies. Some important differentiators of inspections as compared to other types of technical reviews are the roles (author, inspection leader, inspector, and scribe) and the inspection process which consists of the steps planning, kick off, individual checking, logging meeting and edit and follow-up. Some examples of inspections are: Checklist-based reading, Usage-based reading, Defect-based reading, and Perspective-based reading

3 Software Quality Characteristics

The quality of the processes is important to deliver high quality software products. However, many factors influence the quality of the product itself, so it is necessary to evaluate and monitor the quality directly in the product, and improve the processes that create them [9].

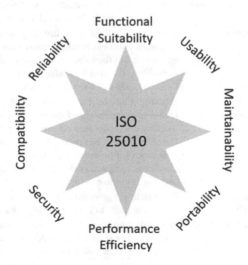

Fig. 1. Quality characteristics of ISO 25010.

In this paper we focus on software product quality. In this context, the ISO 25010 standard defines the quality model that is considered the cornerstone of a product quality evaluation system. The product quality model defined by ISO 25010 is composed of eight quality characteristics, which determine the properties of a software product for its evaluation [5]. Figure 1 shows the eight quality characteristics of the ISO 25010 standard. A short description of these quality characteristics and a listing of the corresponding sub-characteristics, based on the definitions contained in [5], follows in the Table 2.

Table 2. Description of ISO 25010 quality characteristics

Characteristic	Short description	Sub-characteristics
Function Suitability	Degree to which a product or system provides functions that meet stated and implied needs when used under specified conditions	Functional Completeness, Functional Correctness and Functional Appropriateness
Performance Efficiency	Represents the performance relative to the amount of resources used under stated conditions	Time Behavior, Resource Utilization and Capacity
Compatibility	Degree to which a product, system or component can exchange information with other products, systems or components, and/or perform its required functions, while sharing the same hardware or software environment	Co-existence and Interoperability
Usability	Degree to which a product or system can be used by specified users to achieve specified goals with effectiveness, efficiency and satisfaction in a specified context of use	Appropriateness, Recognizability, Learnability, Operability, User Error Protection, User Interface Aesthetics and Accessibility
Reliability	Degree to which a system, product or component performs specified functions under specified conditions for a specified period	Maturity, Availability, Fault Tolerance and Recoverability
Security	Degree to which a product or system protects information and data so that persons or other products or systems have the degree of data access appropriate to their types and levels of authorization	Confidentiality, Integrity, Non-repudiation, Accountability and Authenticity
Maintainability	Degree of effectiveness and efficiency with which a product or system can be modified to improve it, correct it or adapt it to changes in environment, and in requirements	Modularity, Reusability, Analyzability, Modifiability and Testability
Portability	Degree of effectiveness and efficiency with which a system, product or component can be transferred from one hardware, software or other operational or usage environment to another	Adaptability, Installability and Replaceability

4 Survey Plan

4.1 Main Goal and Scope

The main goal of our survey is to gather initial evidence, through expert opinion, about the suitability of V&V methods to address ISO 25010 software product quality characteristics. Using the GQM (Goal Question Metric) definition template [11] this goal can be stated as: **Analyze** V&V methods **for the purpose of** characterization **with respect to** their suitability for addressing ISO 25010 software quality characteristics **from the point of view of** experts in the area of V&V **in the context** of the software engineering research community.

4.2 Population

Following the advice of deciding upon the target population based on whether they are the most appropriate to provide accurate answers instead of focusing on hopes to get high response rates [8], our population of V&V experts was sampled by selecting PhDs in software engineering that are active in at least one of the following software engineering and V&V program committees: ICSE, ICST, ESEM, SEAA-SPPI, and SWQD. Additionally, each survey participant should have at least one publication within the last 5 years directly related to V&V methods. We believe that this strategy allows effectively reaching a sample of V&V experts from the software engineering research community.

4.3 Survey Questions

The survey was designed with only two very direct questions. The intent of keeping the design simple was to allow the experts to answer within a reasonable timeframe.

Q1: To what extent do you agree that the following V&V methods can be applied to address the listed quality attributes?

This question was structured as a table crossing the selected V&V methods (cf. Sect. 2) against the ISO 25010 quality characteristics (cf. Sect. 3). The researchers should provide their answers filling each cell with a number corresponding to a *Likert* scale (1- Disagree, 2- Partially Disagree, 3- Partially Agree, 4- Agree, and N- Not Sure).

Q2: Complete the list by rating any other V&V methods that you believe could be applied to address one or more of the listed quality attributes.

This question was optional and provided to allow the expert to suggest and evaluate other V&V methods, not included in our initial list, that he considers relevant.

4.4 Metrics

Likert scales (1- Disagree, 2- Partially Disagree, 3- Partially Agree, 4- Agree, and N- Not Sure) were used for assessing the V&V methods against the quality characteristics in both questions. The aggregated metric on the agreement for each method/quality-characteristic set was obtained using the median value, which can be safely applied to *Likert* scales [11].

4.5 Execution Strategy

The execution strategy consisted of identifying the population sample according to the strategy and distributing the survey instrument via email. Due to the format of the questions, the survey was provided by e-mail as an MS Word attachment. Participants should answer the survey within 15 days.

4.6 Statistical Techniques

The aggregation of the responses for the set of answers was conducted using the median value. Additionally, the Median Absolute Deviation (MAD), representing the degree of concordance between the experts, was analyzed to further understand the representativeness of the median for the sample. Statistical visualization features to provide an overview of the results include tables and a bubble plot crossing information of V&V methods and quality characteristics.

4.7 Instrumentation

The questionnaire instrument had a title, a short description of the research goal, a note of consent stating that individual data will be handled anonymously, followed by the two questions. Additionally, as supporting documentation, short descriptions of the V&V methods and the ISO 25010 quality characteristics were also provided as an appendix.

4.8 Validity Assessment

Throughout the process of planning the survey according to [11], we identified some threats. Table 3 lists these potential threats and how we treated them in our survey. One of the main mitigation strategies was validating the instrument by asking other individuals to answer the survey, as part of a pilot study, before handing it over to the

Table 3. Threats and treatment

Threats	Treatment
Bad instrumentation	Revision and evaluation of the questionnaire about the format and formulation of the questions. Running a pilot study
Inadequate explanation of the constructs	Revision and evaluation of the questionnaire about the format and formulation of the questions. Running a pilot study
Doubts of the experts on the purpose or on specific definitions	Including the research goal explanation and adding support information on the V&V methods and ISO 25010 quality characteristics
Measurement and results reliability	Using medians to aggregate individual Likert scale entries. Using the median absolute deviation to check on the agreement among the experts
Statistical conclusion validity	This threat strongly depends on the sample size. A mitigation that could be used is running future survey replications and aggregating the results

experts. This also allowed us to understand that, while we tried to keep it is simple as possible, answering the questionnaire still requires at least 20 min.

5 Operation

Our population sampling strategy, described in the Subsect. 4.2, allowed us to identify 145 candidate subjects (PhDs in software engineering, active in one of the selected program committees, and with relevant publications on V&V methods). The survey was sent to them by e-mail as an MS Word attachment, which could be easily answered by using any MS Word compatible editor. Experts had 15 days to answer the survey. After this deadline the data collection was considered concluded.

At all, 19 experts (response rate of ~13%) from 7 different countries answered the survey. Taking into account the main factors that directly affect the response rate [6]: length of the form (number of pages), sending of the form through e-mail, duration to fill out the form (indeed, some experts mentioned that answering took them much longer than expected from our pilot study) and comparing with similar studies (e.g., [3]), where the response rate is commonly around 10%, we can consider our response rate satisfactory and according to our expectation.

Figure 2 represents the number of responses per country. It can be observed that most of the answers came from Brazil and Austria. This was probably related to the direct relationship of the authors with researchers from these countries.

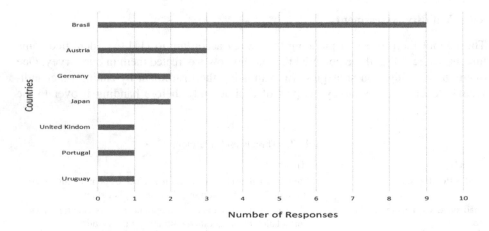

Fig. 2. Number of responses (horizontal axis) per country.

6 Survey Results

The overall results relating the V&V and ISO 25010 quality characteristics are shown in Table 4. The rows contain each of the selected V&V methods, listed from 1 to 19, and the columns show the ISO 25010 software quality characteristics: FS – Functional Suitability, PE – Performance Efficiency, C – Compatibility, U – Usability,

R – Reliability, S – Security, M – Maintainability and P – Portability. The numbers in the cells correspond to the median values of the experts' answers on how suitable the method is for a given characteristic. For the purpose of calculating the median value "N - Not Sure" responses were not considered. The Median Absolute Deviations (MAD) are shown within parentheses.

For the analysis of the survey data, we consider that the method is reported to address a quality characteristic if the median value of the answers of the respondents is greater than or equal to 3. The cells corresponding to these values are highlighted in grey in Table 4. It is possible to observe that, according to the experts, there is at least

Table 4. Suitability of V&V methods to address ISO 25010 quality characteristics.

Methods	FS	PE	C	U	R	S	M	P
1. Ad Hoc Testing	3 (0)	1 (0)	2 (0.5)	3 (1)	1 (0)	1.5 (0.5)	1 (0)	1 (0)
2. Exploratory Testing	3 (1)	2 (1)	2 (0.5)	3 (1)	2 (0)	2 (1)	2 (0)	2 (1)
3. Equivalence Partitioning	4 (0)	2 (1)	1.5 (0.5)	1 (0)	2 (1)	1 (0)	1 (0)	1 (0)
4. Pair wise Testing	3.5 (0.5)	1 (0)	2 (1)	1 (0)	2 (1)	2 (1)	1 (0)	1 (0)
5. Boundary-Value Analysis	4 (0)	2 (1)	2 (1)	1 (0)	2 (1)	2 (1)	1 (0)	1 (0)
6. Random Testing	3 (1)	2 (1)	2 (1)	1 (0)	2 (1)	2 (1)	1 (0)	1 (0)
7. Cause-Effect Graphing	4 (0)	2 (1)	2 (0.5)	1.5 (0.5)	2 (1)	2 (1)	1.5 (0.5)	1 (0)
8. Control Flow-Based Criteria	3 (1)	1.5 (0.5)	1 (0)	1 (0)	3 (1)	2 (1)	2 (1)	1.5 (0.5)
9. Data Flow-Based Criteria	3 (1)	1 (0)	1 (0)	1 (0)	3 (1)	2 (1)	2 (1)	1 (0)
10. Error Guessing	3 (1)	2 (1)	2.5 (0.5)	2 (1)	3 (1)	2 (1)	1 (0)	2 (1)
11. Mutation Testing	3 (1)	1 (0)	2 (1)	1 (0)	3 (1)	2 (1)	1 (0)	1 (0)
12. Operational Profile	3 (1)	3 (1)	3 (1)	3 (1)	3 (1)	2 (1)	1 (0)	2 (1)
13. Usability Inspection Methods	2 (1)	1.5 (0.5)	2 (1)	4 (0)	2 (1)	2 (1)	1 (0)	1 (0)
14. Finite-State Machines	4 (0)	2 (1)	2 (1)	2 (1)	3 (1)	3 (1)	2 (1)	1 (0)
15. Workflow Models	4 (0)	2 (0)	2 (1)	3 (1)	2 (1)	3 (1)	2 (1)	1 (0)
16. Walkthrough	3 (1)	2 (1)	2 (0)	2 (1)	2 (1)	2 (1)	3 (0.5)	2 (1)
17. Peer Review or desk checking	3 (1)	2 (1)	2 (1)	2 (1)	2 (1)	3 (1)	3 (1)	2 (1)
18. Technical Review	3 (0)	2 (1)	2 (1)	2 (1)	2.5 (0.5)	3 (1)	3 (1)	3 (1)
19. Inspection	4 (0)	2 (1)	2 (1)	3 (1)	2.5 (1.5)	3 (1)	3 (1)	3 (1)

one of the selected V&V methods addressing each quality characteristic. Most of the methods address functional suitability.

The MAD represents the agreement between the experts. Figure 3 shows the overall distribution of the MAD values: 32%, 9%, 58%, and 1%, for the MAD values 0 (blue), 0.5 (orange), 1 (grey), and 1.5 (yellow), respectively. It can be seen that these values mainly oscillate in a range between 0 and 1 (except for one element that equals 1.5, concerning using inspections to address reliability). These overall low deviations indicate small differences between the opinions of the experts.

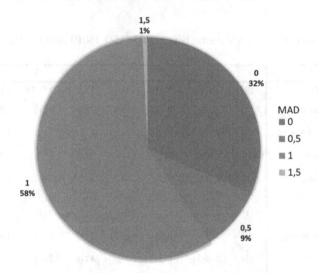

Fig. 3. Median absolute deviations of the answers provided by the experts. (Color figure online)

Figure 4 provides a summary of the relation between the V&V methods and the quality characteristics in a bubble plot. In this Figure, the size of the bubble: small, medium and large, represents the median value: 3, 3.5 and 4, respectively. The colors refer to the MAD value: Blue, Orange and Grey represent the values of 0, 0.5 and 1, respectively. Thus, the large blue plots represent combinations where the experts agree (median 4) with strong consensus (MAD 0) that the V&V method is suitable for addressing the quality characteristic. It is noteworthy that the grey dots, still represent a positive evaluation for the combination (median 3 and MAD 1).

The participants mentioned 20 other (more specific) V&V methods. Among these methods, the ones that were cited by more than one expert were: Model Checking, Penetration Testing, Stress Testing, and Fuzz Testing. It is noteworthy that all methods suggested by more than one expert are automated or semi-automated ones. This indicates that in a future survey trial such methods should probably be included.

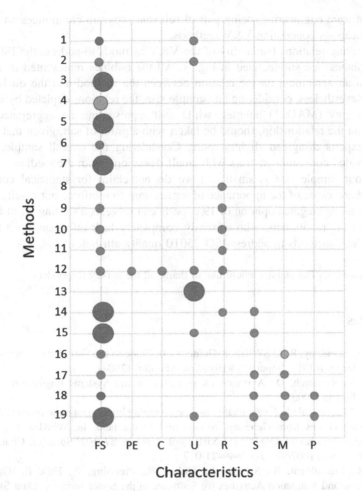

Fig. 4. Map of V&V methods that were considered by experts to appropriately help addressing each of the ISO 25010 quality characteristics. Size of the bubble: small, medium and large, represent the median value: 3, 3.5 and 4, respectively. Colors refer to the agreement (MAD value): Blue, Orange and Grey represent the values of 0 (strong agreement), 0.5 and 1 (still a reasonable agreement). (Color figure online)

7 Concluding Remarks

In this short paper we proposed to establish a relation between a set of V&V methods and the ISO 25010 quality characteristics, based on expert opinions. It is noteworthy that, such relation, while being extremely relevant for research and practice, has not yet been established.

Therefore, we compiled an initial list of V&V methods and carefully selected experts to answer our survey. At all, we received answers from 19 experts, all holding

PhDs in software engineering, being part of relevant program committees and having recent publications concerning V&V methods.

The resulting relations (suitability of the V&V methods to address the ISO 25010 quality attributes) are summarized in Fig. 4. All the bubbles represented in this Figure concern an agreement on the relation between the method and the quality characteristic. Nevertheless, considering our sample size, the relations depicted by the small (median 3) grey (MAD 1) bubbles, while still representing an aggregated expert agreement on the relationship, should be taken with a grain of salt, given that in these cases the experts disagreed slightly more. Considering the overall sample, experts mostly provided consistent answers with small deviations from the median.

While our sample size is small and we do not claim for statistical conclusion validity and are aware of the importance of replications to reinforce our results, we still believe that the aggregated opinion of 19 experts can serve as a starting point for other researchers and practitioners, who currently completely lack information on the suitability of V&V methods to address ISO 25010 quality attributes.

Acknowledgments. The authors would like to thank all the survey respondents.

References

1. Bourque, P., Fairley, R.E.: SWEBOK Guide V3.0, Guide to the Software Engineering Body of Knowledge. IEEE Computer Society, Los Alamitos (2004)
2. Endres, A., Rombach, D.: A Handbook of Software and Systems Engineering. Addison Wesley, Boston (2003)
3. Felderer, M., Auer, F.: Software quality assurance during implementation: results of a survey in software houses from Germany, Austria and Switzerland. In: Winkler, D., Biffl, S., Bergsmann, J. (eds.) SWQD 2017. LNBIP, vol. 269, pp. 87–102. Springer, Cham (2017). https://doi.org/10.1007/978-3-319-49421-0_7
4. Feldt, R., Marculescu, B., Schulte, J., Torkar, R., Preissing, P., Hult, E.: Optimizing Verification and Validation Activities for Software in the Space Industry. Data Systems in Aerospace (DASIA), Budapest (2010)
5. ISO25000 Software Product Quality, ISO/IEC 25010 (2011). http://iso25000.com/index.php/en/iso-25000-standards/iso-25010
6. Linåker, J., Sulaman, S.M., Maiani de Mello, R., Höst, M.: Guidelines for Conducting Surveys in Software Engineering. Technical report Lund University, Sweden (2015)
7. Meyers, G.J., Badgett, T., Thomas, T., Csandler, C.: The Art of Software Testing, 3rd edn. Wiley, Hoboken (2011)
8. Torchiano, M., Fernández, D.M., Travassos, G.H. de Mello, R.M.: Lessons learnt in conducting survey research. In: Proceedings of the 5th International Workshop on Conducting Empirical Studies in Industry, pp. 33–39 (2017)
9. Wagner, S.: Software Product Quality Control. Springer, Heidelberg (2013). https://doi.org/10.1007/978-3-642-38571-1
10. Wiegers, K.E.: Peer Reviews in Software: A Practical Guide. Addison-Wesley, Boston (2002)
11. Wohlin, C., Runeson, P., Höst, M., Ohlsson, M.C., Regnell, B., Wesslén, A.: Experimentation in Software Engineering. Springer, Heidelberg (2012). https://doi.org/10.1007/978-3-642-29044-2

Listen to Your Users – Quality Improvement of Mobile Apps Through Lightweight Feedback Analyses

Simon André Scherr, Frank Elberzhager$^{(\boxtimes)}$, and Selina Meyer

Fraunhofer IESE, Kaiserslautern, Germany
{simon.scherr, frank.elberzhager,
selina.meyer}@iese.fraunhofer.de

Abstract. Companies developing mobile apps face increasing requirements such as short time to market or high quality. Furthermore, users have more influence on apps, as they can easily provide feedback on the product. Consequently, feedback is a valuable source for product improvement. Ideally, this would be done in an automated way. However, because of the limitations of understanding of natural language by machines, this is not possible in a satisfactory way. We have created a quality assurance process that makes use of feedback by applying lightweight analyses in order to enable product managers to take decisions. Some aspects of our process are the inclusion of emojis to reveal emotions, the detection of trends, as well as the derivation of improvement suggestions. With examples from popular apps, we show the practical application of our process.

Keywords: Quality assurance · Apps · Feedback · Product improvement
Emojis

1 Introduction

Software systems are more and more connected. One part of these systems, such as the Internet of Things or software ecosystems, is an increasing number of mobile apps. Apps are becoming more complex and thus need reasonable development and quality assurance efforts to satisfy the users. Users expect defect-free apps with good usability or fast performance. Users are also able to give feedback, e.g., in app stores. Developers should give attention to this as it influences users and may prevent potential users from using it. Furthermore, the pressure on app developers is increasing: Short time to market is important, regular updates are needed, and budgets are often too small.

We argue that user feedback should be considered much more strongly during the development and quality assurance of mobile apps to strengthen the relationship between software-developing companies and the users of their products. They also have to be able to do so fast in order to cope with the release pressure of apps. To enable the consideration of user feedback without increasing a company's workload, we have developed the Opti4Apps approach [1]. In this publication, we focus only on

© Springer Nature Switzerland AG 2019
D. Winkler et al. (Eds.): SWQD 2019, LNBIP 338, pp. 45–56, 2019.
https://doi.org/10.1007/978-3-030-05767-1_4

textual feedback, with a special focus on how to consider emojis used in such textual feedback.

This article is structured as follows: The next section presents our background and motivation for this contribution. Section 3 describes our preparatory work that enabled us to consider emojis for feedback analysis. Section 4 as the main part of our contribution explains our quality assurance process, followed by an evaluation in Sect. 5. The last section concludes the article and presents directions for future work.

2 Background

The Opti4Apps approach [2] was developed as a quality assurance approach that allows companies to include the behavior and written feedback of their users in their quality assurance and development activities. The goal is to improve mobile apps based on different kinds of user feedback. Feedback can be provided automatically (e.g., via a tracking library on the mobile device) or manually (e.g., via users providing feedback in the app store). From a methodological point of view, feedback can comprise app usage data (e.g., usage frequency, or duration), state (e.g., online state), and explicit user feedback (e.g., reviews, bug reports). In [1], we introduced the theoretical foundations for feedback analysis and presented a classification of feedback.

We gained initial practical experience with our approach in an explorative way in [2]. We developed a web-based dashboard prototype, which shows initial analysis results such as word clouds based on textual feedback. With this, we were able to identify important topics in reviews, which gave us ideas about directions for development. However, the consideration of feedback requires a methodology for detecting and processing different data types found in feedback. We described a classification of user feedback [1], where two of the major types are content-based feedback and rating-based feedback. While former one is mostly based on text, its analysis is more complex than that rating-based feedback. While an overall picture of the ratings can be derived in an automated way without major challenges, getting insights into the content part is more complex. The reason is that current methods for analyzing natural language are not mature enough. For example, many text analysis approaches rely on analyzing the sentiment by considering the text. However, these and highly challenging [3]. Ribeiro et al. [4] performed a comparison of state-of-the-art approaches and reported that the quality of these methods varies a lot. Hogenboom et al. [5] argue that results cannot be compared across languages, because the methods do not perform equally.

Even though text analysis methods have not evolved far enough yet to be able to analyze user feedback fully automatically, textual user feedback offers huge potential for product improvement and quality assurance. We put our focus of analyses that do not require a complete understanding of the language during the automated analysis. Data such as star ratings are a reasonable way for an initial analysis, but do not exist everywhere. Feedback usually includes emotions of the users in a written form, often expressed as emojis. This is why we use emojis in our analysis approach.

3 Enabling Feedback Analysis with the Help of Emojis

In this section, we will describe the background on emojis, which are relevant for user feedback analysis, and a model to classify them. To enable us to use emojis for feedback analysis, we performed a survey on the perception of emojis. We will present the key insights of the study, which is explained in detail in [6]. Afterwards we will present an evaluation on the suitability of emoji analysis in practice.

Emojis are colorful pictographs and symbols, for example: ☺, 🐿, ✓ or 🗡. Emoticons are represented by text characters, e.g., :-). Some programs automatically convert these textual representations into a black and white pictograph (☺), or a colorful emoji (😊). For the sake of simplicity, we use the term emoji for both emoji and emoticon in the following. According to Hogenboom et al. [7], emojis are used to simply express sentiment, to intensify the sentiment indicated by the text, or to clarify the text, which prevents misunderstandings [8], e.g. when the writer uses irony or sarcasm. Emojis occur at significant positions [9] of a text.

3.1 Study on the Perception of Emojis

We want to use this indication of emotion for feedback analysis. We began collecting emojis by considering the Unicode standard for emojis and checked the operating systems support. By the time we had conducted the survey, the major operating systems had adopted emoji 4.0 [10]. This version contains 2384 emojis; adding emoticons brings the total to around 3000 elements. We reduced this set by rejecting emojis that are not related to emotions, such as objects (e.g., 🐿), flags (e.g., ▪), letters and numbers (e.g., 🅾), and geometric forms (e.g., ◻). After that, the set still contained 612 emojis.

To decrease the number of emojis further, we combined emojis with similar meanings and put these together in a group. For example, we group skin color and gender variants of an emoji together. Moreover, similar emojis like 😊 and 😊 were grouped together. For each group, we selected one representative. We chose the most neutral emoji in color and gender as a representative or, if this was ambiguous or not possible, the most common emoji as a representative for this group. The choice of representatives as well as the grouping was validated by three researchers. After the reduction and grouping, 99 representatives remained to be investigated further in our survey.

To use emojis for feedback analysis, we need a classification scheme for them. As emojis are related to emotions, we built an emotion model suitable for emojis. We investigated different psychological models proposed by Ekman [11], Lazarus [12], and Plutchik [13]. The model for our survey should be easy to understand without the need to have a psychological background. On the other hand, it should cover everything that can be expressed with emojis. As a consequence, we investigated other sources that use a classification of emotions, like Facebook reactions [14] and IBM Watson's "Natural Language Understanding Service" [15], a solution for text analysis.

Based on these models, we created a model suitable for emojis (see Fig. 1) with the two dimensions *Sentiment* and *Emotion*. In the Sentiment dimension, it distinguishes between *positive*, *neutral*, and *negative*. The Emotion is divided into subcategories and compromises basic emotions. Regarding positive sentiment, the model distinguishes the emotions *happy, excited,* and *funny*. In the neutral category, we also find the emotion *surprised* because it can be either positive or negative. This sentiment also includes the options *really neutral* and *context-dependent if positive or negative"*. In the third sentiment category, the model distinguishes between *angry, scared, sad,* and *bored*.

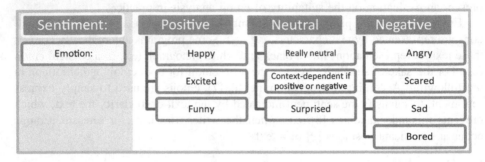

Fig. 1. Emotion model for emojis

With the model and the representatives, we performed a survey to investigate the perception of emojis. The participants were asked to classify the emojis by the sentiment and by emotion (see Fig. 1) that best matches the emoji. We had 53 female and 54 male participants. 101 participants indicated being middle familiar (n = 26) or familiar (n = 75) with emojis.

In our analysis, we selected the sentiment for an emoji if 50% of the respondents gave the same answer. Table 1 shows how well we were able to classify the representatives. Only seven of them could not be categorized, belonging to 21 emojis. The other 92 had an agreement of at least 50% that are 591 emojis in total. We were able to categorize 66 representatives, belonging to 485 emojis, with an agreement of 70% or more.

Table 1. Emoji categorization agreement according to sentiment

Agreement	Sentiment
<50%	*_* ※ :$ 🐷 🐶 ⛰ 🐱
≥50% - <70%	🐨 ✅ @.@ 🐟 X_X 🆗 }:-) 😊 😐 🧍 🏃 :-X 🐶 🐱 🐵 🐔 🐦 🐘 @};- 🐝 >.< 🐷 🐰 ^0^ zᶻ |-O
≥ 70%	O:-) 😂 😆 🍫 </3 -.- 🐍 😌 😎 🐧 :'-(😊 😇 😁 😀 😅 🦄 😞 <3 🎄 D: 😕 :-/ 🍔 :-* 🐵 :D 😢 :'-) (._.) 😊 🍴 📻 🕯 🥚 🐭 🐹 🐰 🐻 🐼 🐻 4 🐤 🐥 🐣 🐔 🐵 😊 😊 :-(😊 💀 :-) 🐮 😊 :-O 😷 🌽 👍 :-P 😠 >_< 😊 😋 😊 ;-) 🐛 🐌

Another finding was that most of the emojis that we were able to categorize according to the sentiment also had a clear meaning in terms of emotion. Table 2 shows only those representatives that we were able to categorize according to sentiment and the percentage to which the participants agreed in terms of emotions. 78 representatives belonging to 512 emojis had an agreement on the emotion level of at least 50%.

Table 2. Emoji categorization agreement according to emotion

Agreement	Emotion
<50%	@.@ 🐛 X_X 😵 :-X 😦 >.< 💀 |-O 😿 >_< 😖 ;-) 🐃
≥50% - <70%	O:-) 🙌 -.- 😺 😻 😽 👽 }:-) 😊 😊 😀 D: :-/ 👌 :D 😊 :'-) 📶 🔋 😠 😡 OK 🐛 😾 🐚 🐌 👐 🕊 👈 👇 @}:- 🙀 😲 ^0^ 💤 😊 👊 💥
≥ 70%	😊 😊 🍎 </3 ✅ 😺 👌 :'-(😊 😊 😊 🙍 🙋 💔 <3 😨 :-* 😊 (._.) 😊 👈 😊 👌 📱 🙆 🙎 ♻ 😊 😊 :-(🐚 :-) 😼 :-O 😊 🌱 👇 :-P 😊

To use our results for analyzing user feedback, the classification of emojis into sentiments and emotions is important. This is shown in Table 3. It turned out that 243 emojis were positive, 131 neutral, and 217 negative. We were not able to classify the remaining 21 emojis of our study, which are distributed over seven groups. You can see the representatives and the number of emojis we were able to classify regarding emotion in the third and fourth column of Table 3. The emojis are labeled with an undecided emotion based on an agreement of less than 50% mentioned above.

Table 3. Categorization of emojis into sentiments and emotions

Sentiment	Emotion	Representatives	#Emojis	Sum
Positive	Happy	O:-) 😊 😺 :-* 😊 😊 :-) 👌 😊 😊 @}:- ^0^ ;-) 😊 😊 😊 👌 ✅ }:-) 😊 :D 😊 <3	166	243
	Excited	🙌 👍	12	
	Funny	👋 😺 😽 😊 🙈 🙉 😊 :-P	34	
	Undecided	😊 😊 🐛 ;-) 🐃	31	
Neutral	Really neutral	😺 OK ♻	3	131
	Context dependent if positive or negative	👌 😊 🙏 👌 📶 😶 👐 👇 👈 👇 💤 😊 🙎	72	
	Surprised	:-O	24	
	Undecided	🙀 |-O @@	32	
Negative	Angry	😠 🍎 👊 😊 👌 😊 🙀	33	217
	Scared	😊 😨 😧 🙀 😊 D:	13	
	Sad	</3 😊 :-(:-/ 🙍 🙎 😭 :-(🌱 😊 😊 (._.)	145	
	Bored	😊 -.-	10	
	Undecided	XX :-X >.< 💀 >_<	16	
Undecided		*_* 💥 $ 🐌 😊 🐃 😾	21	21

In summary, it can be said that people perceive emojis homogenously in terms of sentiment and emotion. Furthermore, the survey shows that the categorization of the emojis does not depend on the age or gender of the participant. These results served as a baseline for our subsequent work of using emojis in the context of feedback analysis.

3.2   Evaluating Emojis for Use in Feedback Analysis

As our survey enabled us to get an understanding of emojis, we investigated whether using emojis is practical for feedback analysis. We checked to which extent feedback analysis done by analyzing star ratings equals feedback analysis done by analyzing emojis. We investigated 178,848 feedback entries of popular apps in the Apple App Store and looked at a mixture of paid and free apps as well as at a mixture of categories to get a heterogeneous group of apps.

We checked whether reviews, containing emojis, showed different distribution of star ratings compared to all reviews. Figure 2 illustrates the distributions and shows that there are only minor differences. The biggest differences were found in the extreme values of the star-rating scale. 30% of all reviews had a one-star rating. The percentage for the reviews with emojis is lower, namely 26%. The percentage of all reviews that have a five-star rating is 45%, and the percentage of the reviews with emojis is 49%. The distribution of all reviews and of the reviews with emojis shows a tendency towards the extreme values of the rating scale. This finding is consistent with previous studies reporting that satisfied and unsatisfied users give more feedback than those who are neutral [16]. Because our focus was on popular apps, it is reasonable that the number of very positive reviews would exceed the number of very negative ones.

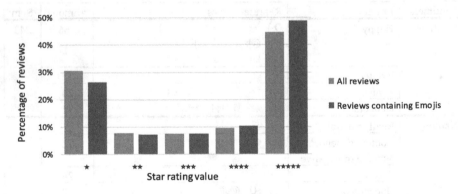

Fig. 2. Distribution across stars of all reviews and reviews with emojis

One of our goals was to explore how much the sentiments expressed by star ratings and by emojis resemble each other. The sentiment expressed by an emoji can be negative, neutral, or positive. A negative emoji gets the sentiment value -1, a neutral one gets 0, and a positive one gets $+1$. We calculated the mean value of sentiments expressed by the emojis and call this value "emotional sentiment" of the review. This means that the emotional sentiment is on a scale between [0, 1]. We calculated the correlation between the ratings and the emotional sentiment by using Spearman's rank correlation coefficient and Kendall's tau. Spearman's rank was 0.680 and Kendall's tau was 0.614. This indicates a strong correlation between the two sentiments and makes emojis suitable as an indicator, similar to star ratings. When using the emotion and not just the sentiment, a more fine-grained result can be obtained compared to star ratings.

4   Rapid Feedback Analysis Process

We have detailed Opti4Apps [2] into a fine-grained process for quality assurance and product improvement (see Fig. 3). This process is as a concrete instantiation tailored to textual feedback. Our primary goal is to enable developers to include feedback analysis without much additional effort, while still being able to improve the product in a substantial manner. This is achieved by including tool support and lightweight analysis, to make fast and well-grounded decisions. The key driver of our idea is that user feedback is collected and analyzed continuously and not only at selected points in time. To realize this, our process uses a mixture of automated, semi-automated, and manual steps. The process contains twelve steps, which can be categorized into three phases: (1) feedback collection, (2) data analysis, and (3) product improvement.

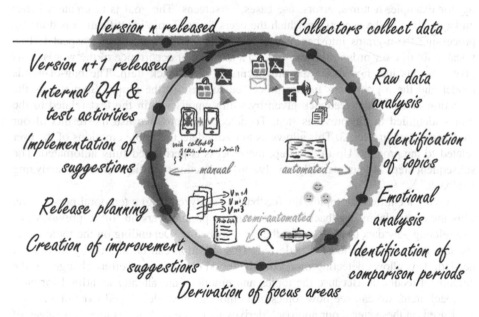

Fig. 3. Process for quality improvement by detecting trends in user feedback

4.1   Feedback Collection and Pre-processing of the Data

After a version of a product is released, feedback data collectors start collecting data from different data sources. These sources can be, for instance, app stores, social media, bulletin boards, or customer support data. Currently, we can crawl data from Apple App Store, Google Play Store, and Amazon Market Place. Crawlers for Facebook and Twitter are currently under development. In addition, we can manually add other feedback, which is used, for instance, add customer support requests.

4.2   Data Analysis

Our raw data analysis calculates how much feedback was captured per source and per period. For data containing rating indicators like star ratings, likes, or votes, this is also analyzed. In addition, the feedback items are related to product variants and versions. To make further steps easier, we apply standard text processing techniques. First of all, texts are lemmatized resulting in having the root forms of the words. Based on that, we remove filler words. Furthermore, we use dictionaries to replace Internet slang terms with their common equivalents. The analysis continues with the creation of an n-gram model of the text and create unigrams and bigrams. Unigram models are based on single words, while bigram models consider a word as well as the next word.

In the fourth step, the approach identifies topics in an automated way. A topic could be, for example, features, errors, use cases, or screens. The goal is to create a better understanding of the aspects on which the users focus. Topic identification is done by processing the n-grams into bag-of-words models that consists of two aspects: (1) a vocabulary of the words in the text and (2) a measure of occurrence of the words. This gives insights into how often a word occurs in a feedback item. The bag-of-words model and the n-grams are further processed to identify the topics. Step five is the detection of emotional feedback given by using emojis within the text related to the topics identified in the previous step. To detect emotions, we use the results of our study described in Sect. 3. This allows us to easily detect possible emotions of the user related to the product. Up to this step, the process is performed fully automated. The subsequent steps at least partially involve manual actions by the user when analyzing feedback.

Having identified the topics, the feedback is analyzed from a temporal perspective. This includes relating feedback from the current product version to the previous one and relating new data to the used for the analysis before. Depending on the topic, other suitable comparison periods are selected. This selection can be altered by the user if needed. This allows detecting mood trends, mood changes, as well as changes in the amount of feedback. Because the topics and emotions are already identified for each feedback item, we can see how topics and emotions have developed over time.

Based on these steps, our approach derives focus areas. A focus area is a subset of the feedback requiring attention. Focus areas themselves are neutral, as they might relate to positive or negative aspects. For instance, a focus area could be the fact that a topic that has been more negative historically changed into something positive due to a well-received change. This would allow the product manager to check whether recent changes of the product are accepted by the users, or if further actions are needed.

4.3 Product Improvement

The product improvement phase of the process starts with the deviation of improvement suggestions for the product. These suggestions focus on problems identified with the product. The suggestions are created based on the focus areas, but also on heuristics that can be applied. Some heuristics do, for example, detect areas where the feedback from the iOS App deviates a lot from that of the Android app, determine whether the amount of positive feedback has dropped under a certain threshold, or report that a certain topic led to an overwhelming amount of feedback. If the improvement suggestion is related to a failure in the product the error is classified and documented. If it is related to changes of the product with respect to new or altered requirements, new requirements are derived as part of regular requirements engineering in the project. Once the suggestions have been derived, each of them is prioritized.

Based on the improvement suggestions and their prioritization, each of them is incorporated into the product's release plan. After the release plan has been updated and the regular project planning has been performed, the suggestions for the next product iteration are implemented. After the implementation phase, the product is subjected to quality assurance. This is done in two ways: (1) as the team would do it without the feedback analysis process and (2) by systematically checking the improvement suggestions being implemented for this version. If the version fulfills the desired quality standard, an update is published manually by the team.

As soon as the improved product is released, the process starts again with the collection step. This enables long-term product improvement by consequently including user feedback. If the issues of the users are addressed quickly enough and their innovative ideas for the product are implemented in an adequate fashion, acceptance of the product will increase and the user base will be more satisfied. The increased satisfaction can be measured again by analyzing the user feedback.

5 Applying Our Feedback Analysis Process

We applied our process, by using our Opti4Apps Dashboard described in [2]. The dashboard was continuously updated and extended. We gained first hands-on experience with feedback captured from the Apple App Store for various apps. In the following, we will show some examples in the form of a post-mortem analysis of feedback collected for Snapchat, Instagram and Tinder.

Snapchat got a huge amount of feedback at the end of June 2017. This was when Snapchat issued an update with a new feature called "Snap Map", where posts and people are displayed on a map. As users did not find this feature intuitive to use [17], Snapchat experienced a drop in ratings and we found an increase in the use of negative emojis. We observed a similar increase on 27 July 2017. The reason for this was a temporary service interruption [18]. We again observed a similar increase in February 2018 that continued for several months, when the app got a major redesign in its UI. News media reported that within several days, more than 800,000 users signed a petition to roll back to the old UI [19]. The feedback had an average rating of 1.3 stars in February 2018 and 1.4 stars in March 2018. More than half of the entire feedback was related to the update. This makes the update responsible for the ratings drop.

We also performed an analysis on Instagram, which experienced two ratings drops in July 2017. Both of them were linked to an increased amount of feedback as well as more negative emojis. The first one was at the beginning of July. At this time, Instagram experienced a short-time bug in the app, which marked accounts deleted by mistake [20]. This prevented the affected users from using the service. The situation at the end of July was related to a partial downtime lasting for about twelve hours [21].

In September 2017, Tinder faced a lot of complaints about the app crashing permanently after installation of an update. This was related to a bug introduced in an app update that was resolved two days later [22]. Even though this bug was only present for two days in the iOS App, the ratings between September and October differed by one star on average. In April, the ratings dropped even further. This time, the drop was related to an issue caused by Facebook changing the way third-party developers can use their API. Tinder was not able to issue an update before the changes became effective and people were logged out of Tinder and could not successfully log in again [23]. Prior to these two issues, Tinder had an average rating of 3.3 stars for reviews in February 2018. In March, the ratings dropped to 2.5 stars, followed by 2.3 stars in April due to the login issue. Both issues were related to a decline in positive emojis and an increase in negative emojis, especially with "sad" and "angry" ones.

The examples demonstrate that changes or problems of a product immediately affect the user feedback. This makes user feedback analysis suitable for observing problems experienced by the users as well as for checking how well updates are accepted by the user base. Depending on the outcome of the analysis, the product can be adjusted within a short amount of time without losing a larger user base. We have seen that even partial service downtimes of only a few hours have a huge impact on the user's perception of the product. We saw that sometimes apps are facing problems due to external changes. As apps are increasingly part of so-called ecosystems, these dependencies and relationships will increase and make app maintenance more complex. This also requires permanent monitoring of user feedback to rapidly change the product, as problems due to external dependencies might be more complex to resolve.

6 Conclusions and Future Work

As part of our research for Opti4Apps, we identified the need for lightweight methods for user feedback analysis. For this purpose, we have defined a quality assurance process. The focus of the process is practical applicability for managers.

One key aspect is the inclusion of emotions into the analysis. Therefore, we performed a survey to link emojis to sentiment and emotions. The results show that people have a homogenous perception of emojis. This allows us to evaluate emojis found in texts and enables a more comprehensive analysis compared to the five-star rating scale. We compared sentiment expressed by the star rating scale and by the emojis in review texts and found that they were strongly correlated. Analyzing emojis in texts allows us to analyze feedback that has no rating-based metrics. In addition, we are able to extract not only a sentiment value from emojis but also detect emotions connected to them.

The results of our emoji survey were included in our process for product improvement by analyzing textual feedback. The central requirements were that it must analyze feedback without much additional effort and that it must be suitable for highly iterative development environments. In addition, we applied our process with examples from popular apps that show that even incidents lasting a few hours have a significant impact on feedback. This implies that fast and continuous analysis of feedback is necessary and making use of this information gives advantages to developers. Even though we only evaluated our approach in the context of mobile apps, the approach itself is not restricted to that. For any software product that is developed in fast increments, rapid analysis of user feedback is beneficial.

We will investigate the usage of emojis in social media feedback and provide a comparison of app store and social media feedback. As more emojis are used in social media [24, 25] compared to our app stores, the importance of emojis might be even higher. As the number of emojis is constantly increasing, we will perform an additional survey on emojis focusing on new emojis and the emojis that we are unable to classify according to emotion based on our first survey.

Acknowledgments. The research described in this paper was performed in the project Opti4Apps funded by the German Federal Ministry of Education and Research (BMBF) (grant no. 02K14A182). We thank Sonnhild Namingha for proofreading.

References

1. Elberzhager, F., Holl, K.: Towards automated capturing and processing of user feedback for optimizing mobile apps. Procedia Comput. Sci. **110**, 215–221 (2017)
2. Scherr, S., Elbertshager, F., Holl, K.: An automated feedback-based approach to support mobile app development. In: Proceedings - 43rd Euromicro Conference on Software Engineering and Advanced Applications, SEAA 2017, Vienna (2017)
3. Hussein, D.M.E.D.M.: A survey on sentiment analysis challenges. J. King Saud Univ. Eng. Sci. (2016)
4. Ribeiro, F., Araújo, M., Gonçalves, M., Benevenuto, F.: SentiBench - a benchmark comparison of state-of-the-practice sentiment analysis methods. EPJ Data Sci. **5**(1), 1–29 (2016)
5. Hogenboom, A., Bal, M., Frasincar, F., Bal, D.: Towards cross-language sentiment analysis through universal star ratings. Adv. Intell. Syst. Comput. **172**, 69–79 (2013)
6. Scherr, S., Polst, S., Müller, L., Holl, K., Elberzhager, F.: The perception of emojis for analyzing app feedback. Int. J. Interact. Mobile Technol. [submitted]
7. Hogenboom, A., Bal, D., Frasincar, F., Bal, M., de Jong, F., Kaymak, U.: Exploiting emoticons in sentiment analysis. In: Proceedings of the 28th Annual ACM Symposium on Applied Computing - SAC (2013)
8. Tauch, C., Kanjo, E.: The roles of emojis in mobile phone notifications. In: Proceedings of the 2016 ACM International Joint Conference on Pervasive and Ubiquitous Computing Adjunct - UbiComp 2016, Heidelberg (2016)
9. Provine, R., Spencer, R., Mandell, D.: Emotional expression online. J. Lang. Soc. Psychol. **26**(3), 299–307 (2007)
10. Unicode: Emoji Keyboard/Display Test Data for UTR #51

11. Ekman, P., Friesen, W.: Constants across cultures in the face and emotion. J. Pers. Soc. Psychol. **17**(2), 124–129 (1971)
12. Lazarus, R.: Emotion and Adaption (1991)
13. Plutchik, R.: A general psychoevolutionary theory of emotions. In: Theorie of Emotions, pp. 3–33 (1980)
14. Brand Resource Center: Reactions. https://en.facebookbrand.com/assets/reactions. Accessed 2016
15. IBM Watson: Natural Language Understanding. Natural language processing for advanced text analysis. https://www.ibm.com/watson/services/natural-language-understanding/
16. Hu, N., Pavlou, P., Zhang, J.: Can online reviews reveal a product's true quality? In: Proceedings of the 7th ACM conference on Electronic commerce - EC 2006, Michigan (2006)
17. Shepherd, M.: How To Use Snapchat's New Snap Map & Become A Social Media Master On The Go. https://www.bustle.com/p/how-to-use-snapchats-new-snap-map-become-a-social-media-master-on-the-go-65941. Accessed 21 June 2017
18. Snapchat Support: Snapchat Support on Twitter. https://twitter.com/snapchatsupport/status/890660305742647297?lang=en. Accessed 27 July 2017
19. Waton, C.: Snapchat update: more than 800,000 angry users sign petition to change redesign. https://www.theguardian.com/technology/2018/feb/13/snapchat-update-redesign-users-sign-petition-undo-new-change-back. Accessed 13 Feb 2018
20. Carman, A.: Instagram bug makes user accounts appear to be deleted. https://www.theverge.com/2017/7/6/15929478/instagram-deleted-accounts-why. Accessed 06 July 2018
21. Crook, J.: Instagram is down for some users. https://techcrunch.com/2017/07/26/instagram-is-down-for-some-users/?guccounter=1. Accessed 26 July 2017
22. Wagstaff, K.: Tinder crashed and now love is dead. https://mashable.com/2016/09/01/tinder-is-down/?europe=true#xXvetVZqJSqU. Accessed 02 Sept 2016
23. Fingas, J.: Tinder suffers sign-in problems following Facebook's privacy changes. https://www.engadget.com/2018/04/04/tinder-sign-in-problems-following-facebook-changes/. Accessed 04 Apr 2018
24. Instagram Engineering: Emojineering Part 1: Machine Learning for Emoji Trends. https://engineering.instagram.com/emojineering-part-1-machine-learning-for-emoji-trendsmachine-learning-for-emoji-trends-7f5f9cb979ad. Accessed 2018
25. Ljubešić, N., Fišer, D.: A global analysis of emoji usage. In: Proceedings of the 10th Web as Corpus Workshop, Berlin (2016)

Agile Software Process Improvement by Learning from Financial and Fintech Companies: LHV Bank Case Study

Erki Kilu[1], Fredrik Milani[2], Ezequiel Scott[2(✉)], and Dietmar Pfahl[2]

[1] LHV Bank, Tallinn, Estonia
erki.kilu@lhv.ee
[2] University of Tartu, Tartu, Estonia
{milani,ezequiel.scott,dietmar.pfahl}@ut.ee

Abstract. A large shift towards the use of agile software development in different industrial sectors is evident nowadays. Financial institutions are not unfamiliar with this tendency since they have the need to respond faster to the changes in their business environments. This is partly due to the new generation of financial technology (fintech) companies that have shown a significant difference in time to market and in speeding up software development. To compete with fintech companies, financial institutions are looking for improving their software development processes focusing on applying agile practices in a better way. This article presents a set of proposals to improve software development in the LHV Bank. The set of proposals has been determined through a literature review and interviews conducted in two leading financial institutions and two fintech companies. The analysis done allowed us to understand the best practices that are currently being applied, how they are implemented, and which ones are suitable for application in LHV Bank.

Keywords: Agile software development · Financial institutions
Fintech companies · Software process improvement

1   Introduction

Large financial institutions have historically relied on waterfall-inspired methods for software development, which have delivered great value for a long time. However, these methods are no longer able to satisfy the current needs in a changing business environment. A shift from waterfall towards agile software development has taken place in the last years due to changes in the competition [3]. Estonia is not unfamiliar with this tendency [16], in particular in the context of financial technology and institutions.

Financial institutions are increasingly investigating software process improvement with agile methods in order to compete with a new generation of companies, also known as financial technology (fintech) companies, that are relying

© Springer Nature Switzerland AG 2019
D. Winkler et al. (Eds.): SWQD 2019, LNBIP 338, pp. 57–69, 2019.
https://doi.org/10.1007/978-3-030-05767-1_5

purely on agile development [14]. In particular, the main question is what financial institutions can learn from fintech companies in order to get their current process more into agile development.

Large financial institutions and fintech companies used to have fundamentally different business models and ways of working. Established financial institutions often have a large number of products that are based on legacy infrastructure whereas fintech companies are focusing only on a small number of niche products using up to date infrastructure. Fintech companies are competing with established financial institutions by offering a subset of products and using their competitive edge in reacting to customer needs and delivering new solutions faster. Compared to established financial institutions, such as banks, fintech companies are focusing only on a few products which they continuously modify responding to customer needs. In other words, they whole organization is agile and, in particular, they are free to develop their software from scratch and with agile development methods.

In order to compete with fintech companies, financial institutions are not only changing their business models but aim at improving their development processes. Like other banks, the LHV bank has already adopted some agile principles and processes. Our study yields improvement proposals that can make LHV's software development processes even more effective and efficient by fine-tuning the adoption of agile principles and practices.

To get a list of proposals for software process improvement (SPI) in the LHV bank, we carried out a review of the literature and conducted interviews with two leading financial institutions and two fintech companies. The interviews with the financial institutions allowed us to understand the best practices they are currently applying and how they have implemented them in their development processes. As a result, we describe eight SPI proposals for the LHV Bank.

This article is organized as follows. Section 2 shows the current software process at LHV Bank. In Sect. 3 we describe the research design. Section 4 shows the analysis and findings obtained. Section 6 discusses the threats to validity and Sect. 7 the conclusions and future work.

2   Context of LHV Bank

LHV[1] is an Estonian bank with 360 employees and more than 133000 clients. LHV bank recognizes itself as an innovative bank with strong investment and entrepreneurship experience. The organizational structure consist of several divisions, where the Retail Banking is the one in charge of product development. It has five product units in charge of 24 different software products related to transactions, investments, and credits, among others. Every product has its Product Owner (PO), yet some POs have more than one product to manage.

There are seven development teams and one R&D initiative team. Each development team is led by a Software Development Unit Manager (SDUM), who

---

[1] LHV Bank web site - https://www.lhv.ee/en/.

usually leads two teams. Development teams consist of 8–12 people: one Analyst, one Lead Software Engineer, three to six Software Engineers and one to three Quality Assurance Engineers. In total, over 70 people are employed in the Information Technology division. The teams in share the responsibility for the development of some products. In case of products with supportive functions, they are divided among several teams.

The product development starts from the product vision created by the PO and approved by the Management Board. The PO is responsible for planning the annual product Roadmap in co-operation with SDUM, where the functionality is included in the Roadmap in terms of Epics. Since the development teams are in charge of more than one product, the POs have to agree on the priorities of Epics in the Roadmap on mutual understanding and agreement.

Every Epic in the Roadmap gets a rough size estimation for resource planning and prioritization. During the development, the time used for different tasks is precisely monitored and reported. On Monthly Planning Meetings, the ways to improve the processes are evaluated. The teams have daily meetings, in which the PO has always the possibility to participate. The Epics are divided into smaller tasks by the SDUM and the Analyst, and the teams have Weekly Backlogs for smaller tasks and bug fixes.

Overall, the setup of the teams and work processes at LHV follows the Scrum [15] method to a large extent. In addition, it has borrowed the elements from XP and Lean Software Development methods well [12]. The bank has a relatively strong visualization culture, where all teams are keeping track of the tasks using the visualization principles typically applied in Kanban [6,12].

3   Research Design

We used a multi-method approach including a literature review and interviews with two leading financial institutions and two fintech companies to derive a list of proposals for software improvement in LHV Bank.

3.1   Participants

The companies for the interviews were chosen from Estonia with the aim to assemble a set of companies with different characteristics. The main criteria for choosing the companies were the following: (a) the company is large enough and well-known; (b) the company has its own in-house software development organization; (c) the decisions taken in different stages of the development processes must be done by the company itself; (d) the company is or has been lately in the fast growth stage; (e) the company has entered other markets in the Baltics, UK, Europe or World in general.

The interviews were done with the following companies: *Swedbank*[2], *Bigbank*[3], *TransferWise*[4], and *Monese*[5]. The interview questions can be found in the appendix of Erki Kilu's MSc thesis[6].

Table 1 summarizes the profile of the companies interviewed. It is worth noting that the companies that have started in the last five years, use agile practices since the beginning. On the other hand, the companies with longer history, have started to take agile practices into use more systemically just in the last three to five years.

Employees playing different roles and with different level of expertise were selected for the interviews. In particular, the employees who agreed to be interviewed were the CTO's, VP's of Engineering and Engineering Leads, who have worked in the companies since the beginning or at least over ten years.

Table 1. Profile of the companies interviewed.

Company	Main markets	Years in activity	Employees	IT employees
Swedbank	Baltics	27	2300	500
Bigbank	Baltics, Europe	12	450	100
TransferWise	UK, Worldwide	7	1200	240
Monese	UK, Europe	3	100	30

4 Results

4.1 Findings from the Literature

LF1: Agile is about the mind-set of the whole organization. This finding relates directly to the Agile Manifesto [1]. The first step in moving from waterfall to agile is to bring the customer close to the rest of the parties involved. As a consequence, the interaction between the parties is increased, and the focus shifts from checking the tasks of the developers to serving the customer and getting the right things done [9]. The second principle states that people interactions are more important than processes. Since people with different skills are working together to deliver product features, it is crucial to guarantee the collaboration as well as their enjoyment on what the team is doing [8]. The third principle is welcoming change. It is very important to react to the changes and even failures when something went wrong. The team has to learn from each iteration and integrate that learning into the next one.

---

[2] Swedbank web site - https://www.swedbank.com.
[3] Bigbank web site - https://www.bigbank.eu/.
[4] Transferwise web site - https://transferwise.com/.
[5] Monese web site - https://monese.com/.
[6] MSc thesis web site - http://comserv.cs.ut.ee/ati_thesis/datasheet.php?id=62042.

In 2015, a research carried out among the financial institutions in Kosovo concluded that the success of implementing agile approaches depends on the structure of the organization and culture. The agile method is about the mindsets of all people in the whole organization. Financial institutions that promote collaboration and a culture of cooperation are in a better standing and accept more easily the transformation from waterfall to agile. In addition, two other attributes from culture, i.e., control and competence, are needed for a successful transformation [4].

LF2: Different agile methods and practices should be combined. Early thinking in agile software development focused on detailed activities, complemented by small and self-contained teams. Over time, it has become clear that the large proportion of software development problems are caused by the poor process management in general. Agile software development is not anymore only about the work division inside a small team, but rather about managing the whole development process. The full benefits of being agile can be achieved only with engaging management and business people [7].

Scrum has helped agile software development teams to organize and become more efficient. In addition, Lean methods like Kanban are extending these benefits. It has been argued that many implementations of Scrum suffer from the same problems that traditional project management methods, and even that it is difficult to manage Scrum without Kanban. Adopting Kanban is an appropriate way to enhance Scrum [12]. In fact, the term Scrumban appears in the literature more often in the recent years, referring to the application of Kanban within a Scrum context [12]. In 2016, the Scrumban concept was efficiently implemented in a large bank in the USA. Although the bank was in agile transformation already for years, it still struggled on slow and unreliable delivery of work. The reason for that was that the bank focused on improving the individual components of the delivery process, but not the entire system [12].

LF3: Agile training enables organizations to a better implementation of the practices. The training on agile is one of the success factors for implementing agile software development [9]. Organizations that provide training to the teams are having more successful implementation of the practices than organizations that do not provide that. The training enables organizations to develop know-how and prepare better for the implementation of the methodology. As in any other project, the support and involvement of the management level improves the success of every business project. However, the larger it is, the more complex it becomes to manage the agile software development [9]. In 2014, the Scandinavian bank Nordea decided to renew their digital banking platform and use agile development methodology to achieve that. As the organization and project were large enough, Nordea decided to use SAFe framework for that purpose. In total, 80 people were trained and the Agile Release Train formed of them consisting of five Agile Teams of development. The bank itself has concluded that proper training was vitally important to start with the project in the right way. The bank stated that the delivery system improved significantly [11].

LF4: Following agile principles in full brings the success in SPI. During 2004–2007, a financial institution KeyCorp made the transition from waterfall to agile software development. One of the main changes was that project managers were turning into Scrum Masters, where development team started to see he/she as another team member [17]. In 2009, the Australian financial institution Suncorp implemented a major system replacement using agile iterative method. One of the main lessons learned was that although unstable and changing requirements are one of the key benefits of agile, it cannot be seen as a way to increase the scope of the project without impacting on time, quality and budget [2]. In 2010, a Danish bank Jyske Bank experienced a problem the planning. The developers felt that preparing planning was like falling back into waterfall approach and they were tagged as old-fashioned [18]. Agile methods do not pay enough attention to agile testing. But the reality is that testing is a crucial part in the whole software development process. It is important to start testing as early as possible and the testing should be run very frequently, even before every source code integration and definitely before every release. Automated tests with relevant tools make more sense as these use less resources and time that is critical in the agile development. To avoid the problems that weak communication between developers and testers may rise, they both should work in the same open space area. Full integration of developers and testers is a productive choice. In agile development, the test plan cannot be fixed. It is important to modify the test plan adequately to the changes in requirements and problems appearing in development [5].

4.2   Findings from the Interviews

IF1. A modular system architecture and microservices are prerequisites for applying agile practices. The system architecture was pointed out by each company as the main success factor for applying agile practices. If the system architecture is monolithic and a large part of the system is built as a single system, applying agile practices is a difficult task. Therefore, the companies pay special attention to a system architecture where the system is composed of smaller modules, where microservices are used as the main software development technique. Although all of the companies said that their new systems are built up using microservices, three of them admitted that they are still having also a monolithic legacy platform. Two of them are in the process of completely changing or splitting up the legacy code into smaller parts.

IF2. Common objectives of team members are important for managing the team. The interviews showed that common objectives of team members are of utmost important. The teams should be fully responsible for their product, both from the business and development perspectives. In a typical setup of a fintech company, the products or features are divided into teams that share common customer support and operations divisions. Such setup allows the teams to set their own business objectives, including not only the development of the product but also the sales targets.

As for setting the objectives and measuring the outcomes, one company uses the Objectives and Key Results (OKR) management tool[7]. The OKR framework [10] allows companies to define targets at different levels such as company, team and personal levels with the aim to increase the visibility of goals inside the organization. The use of a management tool to set the objectives of the teams also serves to measure the team results. However, the focus should not be longer whether the individual developer's productivity is sufficient but instead whether the team is producing the right product and achieves its business goals. In fintech companies, all team members are measured by reaching the same business objectives. That is a crucial factor to amalgam individual team members into a single team that is working under the banner of the same objective.

IF3. Cross-functional can cover the full development cycle of a product. All companies said that they are using the Scrum framework with modifications according to their individual needs. Teams consist of a Product Owner, 4–8 Developers/Quality Analysts and 1–3 other positions that are necessary for the development of specific products. This way, companies establish cross-functional teams, i.e., teams that have all skills to develop a product.

The larger and more mature companies have also a Scrum Master position, sometimes named Project Manager or Product Engineering Manager. Smaller companies do not have a separate Scrum Master position and instead transfer that role's tasks to the Product Owner or Lead Developer. The practices used for software development are tailored according to the level of experience of the team. Mature teams follow the practices proposed by Scrum whereas less experienced teams are allowed to use just Kanban. However, most of the companies admitted that they are also using elements from Kanban on company level or in Scrum teams. This is done in order to track and visualize the current tasks in process and to manage the work in progress.

IF4: A 'Responsiveness to changes' culture is a key element. All the companies repeatedly pointed out that the agile development process should take into account the changes happening in the process of developing a product. For this reason, they use the concept of minimum viable product (MVP). A MVP is a product that has only the most important features that solves the problem for the customer. A MVP gives early feedback about the product directly from the customer and is a valuable input to developing the product further. If the MVP satisfies the customer, it can be developed further; otherwise, the product can be changed quickly [13]. From most of the interviews, it came out that as financial services are regulated more than any other service. For this reason, the MVP is organized in stages. In the first stage (Alpha), the MVP is usually given into use internally to a limited or the whole staff of the company. Just after that, the MVP in the second stage (Beta) is given into use to the limited or whole final customers. If the MVP survives the Beta stage, it can be launched as a new product for customers.

---

[7] OKR product site - https://weekdone.com/resources/objectives-key-results.

It is important to build up a culture of 'Responsiveness to change'. All companies interviewed brought out that the key factor here is the constant exchange of information. The companies often have quarterly or monthly meetings, where the management is giving the business overview and directions and the teams are giving the overview of their activities or products features under development. The culture of closing the products or cleaning the product backlogs is strongly supported in the companies.

IF5: Automated testing accelerates the agile development process. The companies put much attention on how to reduce the time and resources spent on quality assurance of the code. In fintech companies, the developer and quality assurance positions are merged and the companies rely on the tests that have been done by the developers. On the other hand, the larger financial institutions have a separate quality assurance position to fulfill the regulatory requirement of reviewing the code based on the four-eyes principle.

In any case, all the companies stressed the importance of having automated testing process in place. Regression testing was mentioned as the most common software testing technique used. In one company, also Test Driven Development (TDD) as a practice from XP is used.

IF6: Autonomous release processes give independence to teams. All of the companies raised the issue of having an autonomous release process. This process gives independence to teams since they can launch the new products or features when they decide. The previous release process became the bottle neck for teams and the companies have just recently taken into use independent release processes to fasten the launch of the development done. For that, the companies have built their own solutions or bought ready-made orchestration software from the market.

Autonomous release processes give teams the full authority to develop and launch new products or features. As a consequence, the whole process becomes faster because the team does not depend on other resources. In case of bug fixing, the team can fix the reported bugs independently. The teams can decide whether the new feature is made available to all or part of the customers.

5   Proposals

After analyzing the literature and the key findings from the interviews, we generated a list of proposals that might help improve the current software processes at LHV Bank. The following proposals have been prioritized according to their potential of being implemented immediately and not having to wait for a long-term, comprehensive initiative.

P1: Introduce agile management culture organization-wide. Based on LF1 and interviews in general, it can be concluded that being agile is not just about software development but about the mind-set of the whole organization. In small companies, it really covers everyone from the management to the customer support. In larger financial institutions, it is about the management, product management and IT. It can be even said that agile methods are becoming the new management style and culture of the new generation financial institutions.

What originally started from technology-driven companies can also be applied to other types of companies, including financial institutions. Also in financial institutions software technology is playing a larger and larger role every year. All signs indicate that it is time to change the management principles in financial institutions. Instead of rigid silos of business and IT, an organization-wide agile culture that is joining teams should be considered.

In LHV Bank, agile methods and management culture should be introduced to the management on a broader scale. It might be a larger cultural change, but it is worthwhile to try a more decentralized and less controlling management style in general. Since financial institutions usually develop in-house software and not outsourced, they are becoming more like technology companies with high focus on product and software development. Therefore, it is important that financial institutions at all management levels have a good understanding about the agile methods and practices.

P2: Organize relevant trainings. Based on LF3, it is important to have a proper training methodology for the whole organization to increase the knowledge of how to implement more and better agile practices in financial institution. In LHV Bank, when introducing the agile principles, the relevant trainings should be organized and building up the knowledge base should be taken seriously. Learning from other practitioners from the financial sector would add extra value in the learning cycle. The training should take into account the differences of financial institutions as much as possible.

P3: Assemble concrete teams for products. Based on IF3, the agile organization in the financial institutions has to be structured along cross-functional teams. The teams, as smaller units, are responsible for their own product and process from the very beginning until the very end. This is the key to increase development speed.

In LHV Bank, there whole organization structure should be revised with the aim of building more cross-functional consisting of POs and developers with various skills. To avoid conflicts abouts which product gets the highest priority in development teams in charge of 3 to 4 products, the number of products should be reduced by consolidation, as well as the number of business divisions.

P4: Set common business objectives for team members. Based on IF2, it is critical to have a set of common objectives for team members. In the LHV Bank, common objectives can be set for each team. In financial institutions, it is even easier to do this as the whole organization is already having a high level of financial literacy. Usually, financial institutions are project oriented in developing their business. Such culture helps to set and follow the objectives of the teams more easily.

The objectives have to be both quantifiable and qualitative. At least basic business objectives should be set for each team member. For example, if the bank is planning to release a new credit product, the team should set the objective of launching it by the given deadline as well as selling a given number if credits with the help from Marketing and Customer Support. Such objectives will make the whole team more interested in the actual viability of the new product and react quickly to changes, if something needs to be improved for the customer.

P5: Give more autonomy to the teams. Based on IF4, being responsive to changes is a key element in the agile development of financial institutions. In addition to having objectives, the teams should also have the power and autonomy to work towards achieving these objectives.

In LHV Bank, more autonomy should be given to teams by increasing their decision power over their products. Although the financial budget of the team is limited as the number of team members is fixed, the power should be given over the decisions. For example, by letting the team decide what kind of product features to develop, in which order, and at what time the features have to be developed. Giving more autonomy to the teams will ensure that the whole development is moving to the direction of continuous delivery. The autonomy should be given not only to the PO but also to the SDUM. The people playing these roles have to feel that they are working for achieving the common objectives and they have the power and resources to do that. This way, these roles will encourage people to start a new product as a MVP and test it on the real customers, rather than developing anything new.

P6: Review the elements of the agile development method used. Based on LF2 and LF4, each financial institution should find its own way to agile development. Following a specific method might not suit a specific organization. Combining elements of different agile methods will give the best result for a financial institution. However, to support the changes in the process, the organization has to be open minded. Based on IF5, it is important to have as much automated testing as possible to reduce the time spent on manual testing for each change on the software.

In LHV Bank, practices from Scrum, XP, Lean Software Development and Kanban are currently used. However, the whole development process should be reviewed by learning from not only the latest best practices of other financial institutions but also the organizational experience. Including practices such as refactoring and regression testing is essential to decrease the time on testing and to increase the reliability of the systems. At the same time, financial institutions have to guarantee that the code is reviewed based on the four-eye principle. This issue can be solved by applying peer review practices.

P7: Automate the release process. Based on IF6, autonomous release process gives the independence to the teams in financial institutions. It is one the factors of speeding up the development by making the releasing phase shorter since the team is able to react to the bugs faster. In LHV Bank, the releasing process needs to be improved. The current process requires much manual work and involves people from different departments. The whole release process should be redesigned and a suitable information systems taken into use for that. Although the priority of automating the release process is not high in this list, it can actually be done as one of the first things in parallel with the previous proposals.

P8: Use more modular system architecture and microservices. Based on the IF5, the agile practices can be applied in the best way if the financial institution have a modular system architecture. The trend to address modular architectures is using microservices. In LHV Bank, the first core system of the bank accounts was developed already 20 years ago and it has remained the basis for most of the main banking services. Although the new modules of the system have already been built separately, these are still relatively large and do not enable different teams to work on the same component at the same time. Therefore, it is important that in the future, the bank's infrastructure will move towards smaller components and microservices. That will increase the speed in the development of the components.

6 Threats to Validity

There are several threats to validity in this study that we aimed to mitigate.

Construct Validity. Our proposals are based on both a literature review and interviews. The questions discussed in the interviews might have been understood differently by the interviewees. To mitigate this threat, we let a person not involved in the study review the questions.

Internal Validity. The study might give a subjective overview of the product development, IT development and delivery processes of the LHV Bank. This is partly due to the fact that the LHV Bank is a highly regulated institution and for security reasons does not allow to disclose descriptions of all their information systems in a very detailed level.

External Validity. The findings from the interviews were based only on four companies. Although the companies interviewed have different sizes and different levels of maturity, all of them have Estonian roots and their main development is done in Estonia. It might be possible that the companies in other countries or regions worldwide implement different agile practices.

7 Conclusions and Future Work

We present a set of proposals for software process improvement using agile methods for the LHV Bank case. We sketched the currently used software processes at the LHV Bank and pointed out the main improvement areas through a set of proposals. The proposals were based on a literature review and interviews conducted.

Although agile methods and practices have already been used in the software development of the LHV Bank for several years, the proposals listed might allow the organization to implement agile practices in a more powerful way and also across the whole organization. Being agile is relevant not only for managing the software development but also for managing the whole organization.

Once we have established a list of proposed changes, future work will be to implement the proposed changes at the LHV Bank. The implementation plan of proposed changes will be drawn, the resources committed and the execution done. Following the implementation, we plan to evaluate the effects in order to determine whether the improvements were indeed successful.

Acknowledgements. This research was supported by the institutional research grant IUT20-55 of the Estonian Research Council.

References

1. Beck, K., et al.: Manifesto for agile software development (2001)
2. Couzens, J.: Implementing an enterprise system at Suncorp using agile development. In: Australian Software Engineering Conference: ASWEC 2009, vol. 20, pp. 35–39 (2009)
3. Dingsøyr, T., Nerur, S., Balijepally, V., Moe, N.B.: A decade of agile methodologies: towards explaining agile software development. J. Syst. Softw. **85**(6), 1213–1221 (2012)
4. Harjrizi, E., Bytyci, F.: Agile software development process at financial institution in Kosovo. IFAC-PapersOnLine **48**(24), 153–156 (2015)
5. Jureczko, M.: The level of agility in testing process in a large scale financial software project, software engineering techniques in progress. Oficyna Wydawnicza Politechniki Wroclawskiej, pp. 139–152 (2008)
6. Kniberg, H., Skarin, M.: Kanban and Scrum - Making the Most of Both (2010)
7. Kyte, A., Norton, D., Wilson, N.: Ten Things the CIO Needs to Know About Agile Development. Gartner, United States of America (2014)
8. Ladas, K.: Scrumban and Other Essays on Kanban Systems for Lean Software Development. Modus Cooperandi Press, Seattle (2008)
9. Livermore, J.: Factors that significantly impact the implementation of an agile software development methodology. J. Softw. **3**(4), 31–36 (2008)
10. Niven, P.R., Lamorte, B.: Objectives and Key Results: Driving Focus, Alignment, and Engagement with OKRs. Wiley, Hoboken (2016)
11. Nordea, A.: Uniform Heartbeat with Help from Scaled Agile Framework and IJI. Ivar Jacobson International SA (2015)
12. Reddy, A.: The Scrumban [R]evolution: Getting the Most Out of Agile, Scrum, and Lean Kanban. Pearson Education Inc., Boston (2016)
13. Ries, E.: Startup, The Lean: How Today's Entrepreneurs Use Continuous Innovation to Create Radically Successful Businesses. New York (2011)
14. Romanova, I., Kudinska, M.: Banking and fintech: a challenge or opportunity? Contemp. Stud. Econ. Financ. Anal. **98**, 21–35 (2016)
15. Schwaber, K., Beedle, M.: Agile Software Development with Scrum, vol. 1. Prentice Hall, Upper Saddle River (2002)
16. Scott, E., Pfahl, D., Hebig, R., Heldal, R., Knauss, E.: Initial results of the HELENA survey conducted in Estonia with comparison to results from Sweden and worldwide. In: Felderer, M., Méndez Fernández, D., Turhan, B., Kalinowski, M., Sarro, F., Winkler, D. (eds.) PROFES 2017. LNCS, vol. 10611, pp. 404–412. Springer, Cham (2017). https://doi.org/10.1007/978-3-319-69926-4_29

17. Seffernick, T.R.: Enabling agile in a large organization our journey down the yellow brick road. In: 2007 Agile Conference (AGILE) (2007)
18. Svejvig, P., Nielsen, A.: The dilemma of high level planning in distributed agile software projects an action research study in a Danish bank. In: Šmite, D., Moe, N., Ågerfalk, P. (eds.) Agility Across Time and Space, pp. 171–182. Springer, Heidelberg (2010). https://doi.org/10.1007/978-3-642-12442-6_12

Software Testing

Why Software Testing Fails: Common Pitfalls Observed in a Critical Smart Metering Project

Stefan Mohacsi[1] and Rudolf Ramler[2] 📧 iD

[1] Atos IT Solutions and Services GmbH, Siemensstrasse 92,
1210 Vienna, Austria
stefan.mohacsi@atos.net
[2] Software Competence Center Hagenberg GmbH, Softwarepark 21,
4232 Hagenberg, Austria
rudolf.ramler@scch.at

Abstract. Over the last decades a considerable share of software engineering research has been dedicated to the area of software testing. Still, however, testing often fails or causes major problems in practice. In this paper we present insights and experiences from a large project in the energy sector. The obligatory switch from analog energy meters to smart metering technology poses a big challenge for many energy providers. Apart from technical issues concerning meters and transmission technology, the adaption of the internal business processes together with the development of backend software can turn out to be more difficult than expected. The criticality, size and complexity of the analyzed project are reflected in software and system testing, where the underestimated effort, mistakes, and wrong decisions caused serious difficulties. In our work we describe the observed testing problems and the underlying causes. Subsequently, we compare the identified problems with a catalogue of commonly known testing pitfalls and anti-patterns. The results show that the majority of the observed problems are not new or specific to the studied project. Furthermore, additional candidates for extending the list of common pitfalls are identified. Besides recommendations on how to mitigate the problems in the studied project, we conclude with the general insight that there is a great potential to improve software testing practice by developing measures for early recognition, communication, and avoiding of common mistakes.

Keywords: Software testing · System testing · Test management
Common testing pitfalls · Testing Anti-Patterns · Smart metering

1 Introduction

The news is full of stories about software disasters [1]. The number of reports about software failures has dramatically increased over the last decades. And due to the widespread reliance on software systems and their critical role in our everyday life, failures can have tragic and devastating consequences for affected users, businesses and the general public.

It is commonly accepted that it is not possible to create defect-free software [2]. However, numerous methods and techniques exist for assuring and improving the

© Springer Nature Switzerland AG 2019
D. Winkler et al. (Eds.): SWQD 2019, LNBIP 338, pp. 73–92, 2019.
https://doi.org/10.1007/978-3-030-05767-1_6

quality of software systems, for finding and removing defects, and for reducing the risk of failures. Software testing is the most widely known and most frequently used quality assurance measure for the majority of systems built today [3]. In many projects, testing is also the last and most important line of defense for detecting and removing defects before the software is released. Nevertheless, the numerous reports of software problems clearly show that software testing often fails in practice and, thus, systems with critical defects are released.

In this paper we investigate the research question: *Why does software testing fail?* We consider the testing activities in a project to be "failed" if the goals concerning test effectiveness and/or efficiency have not been met. Ineffective testing means that more defects than expected slip into the deliverable system. If testing is inefficient, more time and effort than expected is required to reach the desired quality level. It is known that many projects invest a huge amount of time and effort in testing, which can accumulate up to fifty percent of the overall project costs [3]. Given that a substantial share of software engineering research is dedicated to the area of software testing [4, 5], providing a huge body of knowledge, one may expect that the underlying causes and reasons have to be exceptionally difficult, wicked problems.

It is surprisingly hard to find answers in the literature, as the majority of the testing literature is focused on recommended best practices and technological solution. Only very few studies investigate problems in real-world software testing. Negative cases are rarely reported. In scientific literature this is known as the file-drawer problem [6]. Instead of publishing negative results, these studies are put in the file-drawer. Similarly, companies and practitioners prefer to report success stories rather than admitting that projects were riddled by problems and failures.

The largest study reporting problems and deficiencies in software testing has been issued by the National Institute of Standards & Technology (NIST) in 2002 [7]. The purpose of this study was to quantitatively estimate the economic impact of inadequate infrastructure for software testing. It showed that inadequate testing methods and tools cost the U.S. economy between $22.2 billion and $59.5 billion annually in terms of expenses due to software nonperformance and failures.

Several years later, empirical studies in software engineering started to explore the problems of software testing in practice. Among the few studies available is one by Martin et al. [8], who conducted an ethnographic study of reasons for "bad practices" in software testing in a small software company. An analysis of the problems in testing practice was performed by Kasurinen et al. [9], based on a survey and interviews with 26 organizations followed by in-depth case studies.

A comprehensive catalogue of 92 pitfalls commonly observed in software and system testing has been compiled by Firesmith [10]. The book describes testing problems, symptoms, and solutions that can be used as a checklist for identifying and preventing costly errors and mistakes in real-world projects. The pitfalls correspond to adverse practices and anti-patterns in testing that have to be avoided or should trigger test process improvement actions. We used this list in our work to evaluate the testing activities, identify issues, and suggest appropriate countermeasures.

In order to provide an answer to our research question, we report the testing problems in a large and critical software-reliant systems project from the energy sector. The obligatory switch from analog energy meters to smart metering technology poses a big challenge for many energy providers. Apart from technical issues concerning meters and transmission technology, the adaption of the internal business processes together with the development of backend software can turn out to be more difficult than expected. The project is considered highly critical as its success or failure has a direct impact on the energy supply infrastructure and therefore on a huge number of people in a Central European region.

At the time we performed this investigation, five years had passed since the first analysis step took place in the project and three years since development had been started. Major parts of the system have been completed, but the project is still far from finishing. It is yet not possible to conclude whether the outcome will be a success or failure in the end. Up to now, however, the project faced major challenges that also included software and system testing, where the underestimated effort, mistakes, and wrong decisions caused serious problems.

The objective of this paper is to identify, analyze and describe the diverse problems in software testing that potentially decrease testing effectiveness and efficiency, cause critical defects to be missed, lead to higher testing costs and effort, tester frustration, and ultimately contribute to project failures. Furthermore, the paper makes the following additional contributions:

- It provides an *industry experience report* sharing insights and lessons learned from software testing and quality assurance in a large and complex real-world project on developing a *smart metering system*, part of our critical energy infrastructure.
- The testing problems observed in the studied project are related to the list of *common system and software testing pitfalls* by Donald Firesmith [10] to analyze which problems are new or project-specific, and which resemble already known issues that could potentially have been avoided. Additionally, candidates for extending the list of known pitfalls are identified.
- The paper contributes to the rare cases of documented *empirical evidence of negative results and failures* that are hardly ever reported in scientific or popular literature, even though it is worthwhile to learn from failure cases and mistakes in order to not repeat them in future.
- Suggestions are made on how to mitigate the observed problems and on how to *improve software testing practice* in general by developing measures for early recognition, communication, and preventing of common mistakes.

The remainder of the paper is structured as follows. Section 2 provides an overview of the studied project and a detailed description of issues and problems encountered in the course of testing during the last years. In Sect. 3 the project is analyzed using Firesmith's catalogue of common system and software testing pitfalls as checklist. In Sect. 4 the results are discussed from different perspectives and compared to findings in the related literature. Section 5 concludes with practical recommendations on how to improve software testing in context of the project and in general.

2 Project Context and Background

2.1 Challenges of Smart Metering

Based on the European Commission's mandate M/441 regarding the standardization of smart meters [11], energy providers in the member states of the European Union need to implement an open metering architecture that allows interoperability and provides customers with the necessary information to optimize their energy use.

As a consequence, energy providers have to replace the existing analog energy meters that are sporadically read by a service technician at the customers' sites with smart meters that are connected to the internet and can thus be read remotely and more frequently. The measured values are transferred via various channels (power line communication, mobile network, fiber optic cable network, even directional radio in remote areas) to a head-end which is typically located at the head office of the energy provider. In the same way, it is possible to send commands, requests, and firmware updates in the opposite direction from the head office to the individual meters.

While setting up and operating the network infrastructure between customer and head-end is a major challenge in itself, the software system required behind the head-end is also far from trivial (Fig. 1). The millions of data values that are regularly received from the smart meters need to be stored and processed. The existing IT infrastructure (customer management, billing, etc.) must be expanded and new interfaces need to be implemented to connect the existing systems (white boxes in Fig. 1) to the new smart metering software (dark gray boxes). A web portal is required that allows customers to view their energy usage profile. The network infrastructure needs to be constantly monitored, managed, and secured against data loss and manipulation. Particular care must be taken to avoid malicious attacks, because a prolonged blackout would have disastrous results for a civilization that is completely dependent on electric energy; an unsettlingly realistic scenario is portrayed in [12].

2.2 Project Background

Energy providers are trying to tackle the aforementioned challenges in many different ways. In the following, we will present insights and experiences from a smart metering transition project in one of Europe's central regions. The role of the authors in the project was that of external consultants and observers who were called in by the customer to identify problem areas and suggest improvements. The authors are not affiliated in any way with the customer or its contractors. Please note that details about the involved parties and the project have to be omitted for reasons of confidentiality.

The studied smart metering transition project was initiated in 2013 with an analysis of the legal requirements and the elaboration of a vision of how a smart meter solution implementing those requirements could look like. Soon it turned out that there were many uncertainties, both from an organizational and technical point of view. It became apparent that smart metering had a huge impact on most existing business processes and that considerable effort would be necessary to find answers to the ever-increasing list of technical questions.

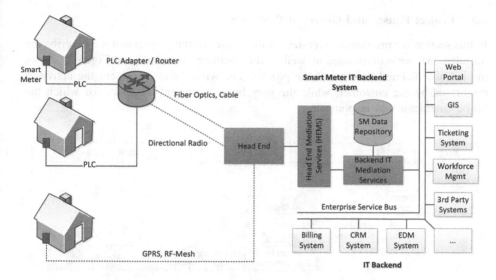

Fig. 1. Exemplary architecture of a smart metering system.

One problem was the lack of documentation of the existing processes. Up to that point, most tasks were performed based on years of experience and organizational structures that had grown in an almost organic way over time. Now, the need for analyzing the impacts of smart metering made it necessary to document these existing processes. The analysis was performed in a number of working groups that included stakeholders from all affected departments who often had very different views on one and the same subject.

After this, the definition of new business processes and the derivation of requirements started. Once again the working groups met to define high-level processes that were gradually refined to requirements. However, since the analysis phase had already caused a delay of an entire year for the smart metering project, there was not enough time to refine the requirements to a level of detail that is usually expected by a programmer or tester. In the end, there were more than 800 requirements, but many of them still too vague for designing a concrete solution or test case. For instance, "the system must check if the received data is complete and plausible" leaves several open questions, e.g., what do "complete" and "plausible" mean in this context?

This set of rather course requirements was used in the invitation-to-tender (ITT) for the IT backend. It was planned that more detailed requirements would be elaborated later on in cooperation with the winning bidder. In the end, the bidder offering at the lowest price won, mostly due to the fact that about 70% of the achievable points were related to the tender price.

Three difficult years have passed since then in which the list of lessons learned has been constantly growing.

2.3   Project Phases and Observed Problems

In this section we provide an overview of the phases of the project and we describe the mistakes that were committed as well as the resulting consequences. Figure 2 shows the initially planned timeline of the project. The white boxes represent the activities performed by the customer, while the gray boxes represent the tasks for which the prime contractor was responsible.

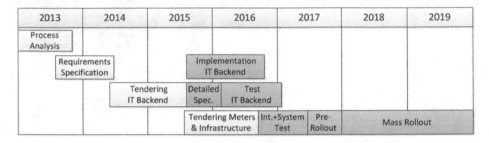

Fig. 2. Initially planned project timeline.

As can be seen from the figure, the prime contractor was not only responsible for the IT backend, but also for performing the test and rollout activities once the meters became available. It can also be observed that no activity "Implementation Meters & Infrastructure" is included in the plan. The reason for this is the wrong assumption that off-the-shelf products would suffice, as it had formerly been the case for analog meters. There was little awareness that certain customizations would be necessary due to the complex relationships and compatibility issues between smart meter firmware, routers, head-end, and backend functionality.

Process Analysis and Requirements Specification. The goals of the first phases were to depict the existing business processes, to analyze the impact of smart metering on them, and to derive requirements from the new adapted processes.

The existing business processes and the impact of smart metering were elaborated about one year too late. The result was a set of requirements with a granularity that was much too course for tendering, development, and testing. For instance, there was a single requirement that encompassed almost the entire functionality of the Meter Data Management, one of the central applications of the smart metering backend.

Requirements were first captured with the tool Enterprise Architect, which – apart from other disadvantages – could not be accessed by non-developers. Thus, the requirements were exported to the tool Jira. Unfortunately, the hierarchical structure of the requirements along with other important information was lost in this step. Also, if a requirement applied to more than one business process, duplicates were created in Jira. The result was a list of requirements accessible by all involved parties, but with the disadvantage that the requirements were not properly usable.

Tendering Stage. The tendering stage was divided into two parts. The first was to identify a prime contractor who would be responsible for the IT backend, but also for the integration and system testing activities. Furthermore, the prime contractor would also be in charge of the rollout of the smart meters to the end customers. A second ITT was issued at a later stage to acquire the smart meters and the required network infrastructure. Several problems can be traced to this stage.

The ITT for the IT backend was published much earlier than the ITT for the meters and network infrastructure. Thus, the contractor for the IT backend did not know at the start which metering technology would be used. This created considerable uncertainty regarding compatibility and design of the IT backend.

In the ITT, 70% of the achievable points were related to the tender price. Only 2% depended on the quality of the proposed test plan. There were no "must" criteria at all for testing. This means that a bidder could win by offering at a low price even if he submitted no test plan at all.

The quality of the proposed technical solution had a weight of only 13.5%, though there were at least several "must" criteria. Nonetheless, a bidder with an inadequate solution could still win if only the price was low enough.

Due to the coarseness of the requirements, it was impossible for the bidders to reliably estimate the effort. In order to win the contract, some of the bidders made overly optimistic assumptions. Soon it became clear that the winner had grossly underestimated the required effort when fixing the offer price. In particular, the contractor had mostly ignored the effort required for testing when doing the estimation.

Detailed Specification. Since the original requirements were much too course grained to be implemented and tested, a refinement phase was necessary in which the prime contractor collaborated with the customer to elaborate the specification.

It was decided that the necessary refinement of the requirements should take place in the tool Confluence in form of Wiki pages rather than using Jira. While this had the advantage of reducing the fragmentation of the requirements, there was the major drawback of losing the traceability between requirements and test cases. Trace links had been established using a direct interface between Jira and the applied test management tool TEMPPO. No such connection existed to Confluence, making it impossible to automatically synchronize the list of requirements with the test cases. Also, the specifications in Confluence were often lengthy pages of plain text, and it was much harder to map a test case to a specific paragraph of a page than to a Jira requirement ID. As a consequence, deriving important metrics such as measuring the achieved test coverage for requirements was only possible with massive effort.

Furthermore, the specification in Confluence was written by different teams. Since there were no shared guidelines regarding style, granularity and nomenclature, the structure and quality of the specified requirements differed widely. Not surprisingly, the same discrepancies could be observed in the test cases that were derived from the specification.

Implementation of the IT Backend. The goal of this phase was to create the IT infrastructure of the backend. Some of its components were standard software products that did not need many alterations. Others required expansions or even had to be implemented from scratch. Creating the interfaces to the existing systems was also a major task. The implementation phase was executed in several iterations, each followed by a test stage.

Unfortunately, the contractor had underestimated the technical complexity and lacked the necessary know-how to implement some components such as the interface to the existing SAP system.

The various components of the IT backend were supplied by different sub-contractors. Each of them had their own standards for implementing the necessary expansions and for performing component tests. In principle, the approach and guidelines specified in the project's test plan (equivalence partitioning, C1 code coverage, etc.) applied to all sub-contractors, but it was hardly ever ensured whether the test plan was followed or not.

This was mainly due to the fact that the contractor's test manager was not independent, but put under pressure from his own company to avoid further delays. Clearly, this created a conflict of interest.

A fluctuation of employees could be noticed in many roles; most prominently that of the project manager, who changed several times. Considering the unrealistic targets specified in the tender and the overall stressful project situation this did hardly come as a surprise.

Testing. While the responsibility for component testing lay with the respective sub-contractors, the prime contractor was responsible for integrating the components and end-to-end testing of the IT backend. Once the smart meters and network infrastructure became available, a second integration stage was required, followed by a test of the complete system and a field test that covered end-to-end scenarios from the end customer households to the databases in the IT backend.

The contractor appointed a test manager who had little experience, both in testing and in managing. When it became clear that a professional test manager plus test team was required, a group of ten external test specialists had to be hired by the contractor. The external testers led to considerable extra costs that had not been planned. After about one year, the contractor's management decided that these extra costs were no longer justifiable and replaced the external specialists with less expensive but inexperienced internal resources. As a consequence, most of the know-how regarding the test approach and test environment was lost.

A large part of the test cases were specified at a coarse level with important details regarding the required configuration, test steps and data missing. Without these details it was often impossible for another tester to understand and execute the tests. Taking into account that the entire test team was replaced after one year, this led to a very serious knowledge gap and subsequent problems in testing activities.

To allow prioritizing in test execution, it was planned to assign a priority value to each individual test case. Unfortunately, this was often not put into practice, mostly because it was not clear from the plain text specifications in Confluence which aspects were important and which were not.

Contrary to the guidelines in the test plan, systematic test design methods such as equivalence partitioning were often neglected, resulting in poor test coverage. In general, the collection of metrics about testing was difficult and only performed superficially. The test manager did not recognize this as a problem, or at least he did not take any counter-measures.

In the schedule of the overall project, there was too little time allocated to testing, especially in the later phases. Main reasons for this problem were the underestimation of the system's size and complexity, and the mindset of the contractor's management, which regarded testing as a cost factor rather than an investment that supports development in accomplishing the specified functionality in the required quality.

In the original test plan, test automation had been emphasized as an important objective. Licenses for automated test execution tools and for a model-based testing tool were acquired, but these tools were hardly ever used. The reasons for this were manifold. One of the main reasons was the instable nature of the requirements. Another one was that the involved testers that had test automation know-how were fully occupied with other tasks – including manual test execution – and never had time to tackle the automation.

Rollout. In a first stage, a pre-rollout should take place during which a few thousand households should be equipped with smart meters. Based on the experiences from this phase, the mass rollout to all end customers should begin.

Due to the numerous problems encountered in the course of the project, the actual rollout of the smart meters to the customers' sites was considerably delayed. At the time this paper is written, it is still unclear when the rollout can start.

3 Common Testing Pitfalls

In this section we further investigate the situation of software and system testing by matching the observed problems to common testing pitfalls as collected and described by Firesmith [10]. He defines *testing pitfall* as "any decision, mindset, action, or failure to act that unnecessarily and, potentially unexpectedly, causes testing to be less effective, less efficient, or more frustrating to perform" [10]. Pitfalls are known "anti-patterns" or "bad practices", which should be avoided as their likely negative consequences can be disastrous for the overall project. However, projects have been found to commonly fall into these pitfalls due to mistakes made by testers, managers, requirements engineers, and other stakeholders.

The book by Firesmith contains a catalogue of 92 testing pitfalls. Each of them has been observed several times on multiple different projects. The pitfalls are grouped into fourteen categories (e.g., pitfalls related to test planning, test processes, unit testing, regression testing) belonging to one of the two high-level categories general testing pitfalls and test-type-specific pitfalls. The book provides a description of each pitfall plus a description of the project setting in which the pitfall usually applies, the characteristic symptoms indicating the possible existence of the pitfall in a project, potential negative consequences, and likely root causes of the pitfall.

Table 1 lists the pitfalls encountered in the studied project. We established the match between Firesmith's catalogue of common pitfalls and the investigated problems in the project based on the pitfall description as well as the observed symptoms and consequences. In this way we identified 29 common pitfalls that clearly affect testing in the studied project.

Table 1. Common testing pitfalls [10] encountered in the studied project.

Test Planning and Scheduling Pitfalls

(1) Test plans ignored	The test planning documentation is ignored (that is, it becomes "shelfware") once it is developed and delivered
(2) Inadequate test schedule	The testing schedule is inadequate to complete proper testing

Stakeholder involvement and commitment pitfalls

(3) Wrong testing mindset	Some testers and testing stakeholders have one or more incorrect beliefs concerning testing
(4) Unrealistic testing expectations	Testing stakeholders (especially customer representatives and managers) have various unrealistic expectations with regard to testing
(5) Lack of stakeholder commitment to testing	Stakeholder commitment to the testing effort is inadequate

Management-related testing pitfalls

(6) Inadequate test resources	Management allocates inadequate resources (for example, budget, schedule, staffing, and facilities) to the testing effort
(7) Inadequate test metrics	Too few test metrics are produced, analyzed, reported, or acted upon, and some of the test metrics that are produced are inappropriate or not very useful

Staffing pitfalls

(8) Lack of independence	The test organization or project test team lack adequate administrative, financial, and technical independence to enable them to withstand inappropriate pressure from the development management to cut corners
(9) Inadequate testing expertise	Some testers, developers, or other testing stakeholders have inadequate testing-related understanding, expertise, experience, or training

Test process pitfalls

(10) Inadequate test prioritization	Testing is not adequately prioritized (for example, all types of testing have the same priority)
(11) Black-box system testing overemphasized	There is an overemphasis on black-box system testing for requirements conformance, and there is very little white-box unit and integration testing for the architecture, design, and implementation verification
(12) Too immature for testing	Objects Under Test are delivered for testing when they are immature and not ready to be tested
(13) Inadequate evaluations of test assets	The quality of the test assets is not adequately evaluated prior to using them
(14) Inadequate maintenance of test assets	Test assets are not properly maintained (that is, adequately updated and iterated) as defects are found and the object under test (OUT) is changed

(continued)

Table 1. (*continued*)

(15) Incomplete testing	The testers or developers fail to adequately test certain testable behaviors, characteristics, or components of the system or software under test
(16) Inadequate test data	The testers or developers fail to adequately test certain testable behaviors, characteristics, or components of the system or software under test
Test tools and environments pitfalls	
(17) Over-reliance on manual testing	Testers place too much reliance on manual testing so that an insufficient amount of testing is automated
Test communication pitfalls	
(18) Inadequate architecture or design documentation	Requirements engineers, architects, and designers produce inadequate documentation (for example, models and documents) to support testing or such documentation is not provided to the testers
(19) Inadequate test documentation	Testers create test documentation that is incomplete or contains incorrect information
(20) Source documents not maintained	Developers do not properly maintain the requirements specifications, architecture documents, design documents, and associated models that are needed as inputs to the development of tests
Requirements-related testing pitfalls	
(21) Ambiguous requirements	Testers misinterpret a great many ambiguous requirements and therefore base their testing on incorrect interpretations of these requirements
(22) Missing requirements	Testers overlook many undocumented requirements and therefore do not plan for, develop, or run the associated overlooked test cases
(23) Incomplete requirements	Testers fail to detect that many requirements are incomplete
(24) Requirements churn	Testers waste an excessive amount of time and effort developing and running test cases based on many requirements that are not sufficiently stable and that therefore change one or more times prior to delivery
(25) Improperly derived requirements	Testers base their testing on improperly derived requirements, resulting in missing test cases, test cases at the wrong level of abstraction, or incorrect test cases based on cross cutting requirements that are allocated without modification to multiple architectural components
(26) Verification methods not properly specified	Testers (or other developers) fail to adequately specify the verification method(s) for each requirement, thereby causing requirements to be verified using unnecessarily inefficient or ineffective verification method(s)

(*continued*)

Table 1. (*continued*)

(27) Lack of requirements trace	The testers do not trace the requirements to individual tests or test cases, thereby making it unnecessarily difficult to determine whether the tests are inadequate or excessive
Integration testing pitfalls	
(28) Unavailable components	Integration testing must be postponed due to the unavailability of (1) system hardware or software components or (2) test environment components)
Regression testing pitfalls	
(29) Inadequate regression test automation	Testers and developers have automated an insufficient number of tests to enable adequate regression testing)

4 Discussion

In the following we analyze and discuss the observed problems in testing and the encountered testing pitfalls from different perspectives to better understand the causes that led to the current situation in the project.

4.1 Pitfall Categories

Firesmith [10] categorizes the pitfalls according to the aspects and levels of testing, where the pitfalls can be commonly observed. He distinguishes 14 different categories. The number of pitfalls per category differs widely, from two to fifteen. The 29 pitfalls we encountered in the project (Table 1) are related to 10 of these categories.

Figure 3 shows the list of categories and the bars depict the number of pitfalls related to them. The *gray bar* represents the *total number of pitfalls* according to the categorization by Firesmith, the *red bar* represents the *number of pitfalls we observed* in the project per category.

Most testing pitfalls we observed concern organizational aspects and test management tasks. Technical problems in testing mostly concern the traceability between requirements and test cases, which however can be attributed to shortcomings in managing the dependencies between the two project phases. This is also reflected in the distribution of the observed pitfalls to categories. *Test process* and *requirements-related testing* are the two categories with most of the observed pitfalls.

These two categories are also rather large categories per se, so it may not be surprising that most of the project's observed pitfalls are in these categories. Yet also when looking at relative numbers (share of pitfalls observed in the project), these categories are among the most affected ones. The top five are *stakeholder involvement and commitment* (two out of two pitfalls observed, i.e., 100%), *requirements-related testing* (78%), *test communication* (60%), *test process* (47%), and *staffing* (40%). 22 of the 29 testing pitfalls are in these categories.

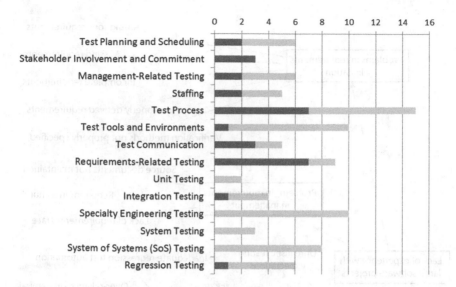

Fig. 3. Total number of testing pitfalls per category as proposed by Firesmith (gray bar) and the number of pitfalls observed in the project per category (red bar). (Color figure online)

4.2 Dependencies and Root Causes

Testing pitfalls were found to be related mainly to organizational and management problems, which can be traced back to similar types of problems at the project level. In this section we will analyze and illustrate the cause-effect chains that led to the observed pitfalls in the studied project.

Figure 4 provides an overview of the 29 testing pitfalls and the related root causes. The testing pitfalls are shown as light-red boxes while the identified root causes are shown as light-blue bordered boxes. The cause-effect dependencies are depicted in the form of arrows connecting these boxes. Pitfalls can often be traced back to more than one cause, and pitfalls also influence each other in the sense that a pitfall causes another one or it increases the likelihood that another one occurs. For the sake of clarity, we reduced the complexity resulting from these dependencies in Fig. 4, which shows only the most influential dependencies.

We were able to identify two root causes for the problems in the project: Firstly, the *lack of experience with large software projects* both on the part of the client and the contractor, and secondly, the *underestimated size and complexity of the system*.

The lack of experience first led to *problems during the elicitation of the requirements* (ambiguous, missing, incomplete, improper, or unverifiable requirements). It also caused *problems with the management of these requirements* (lacking maintainability, traceability, stability). Furthermore, due to the lack of experience there dominated a wrong mindset regarding testing, which led to unrealistic testing expectations, a lack of stakeholder commitment, and an organization in which the test manager depended on the contractor's management.

The combination of both root causes led to an *unrealistic project schedule*, which naturally had severe consequences both for development and testing. Both activities

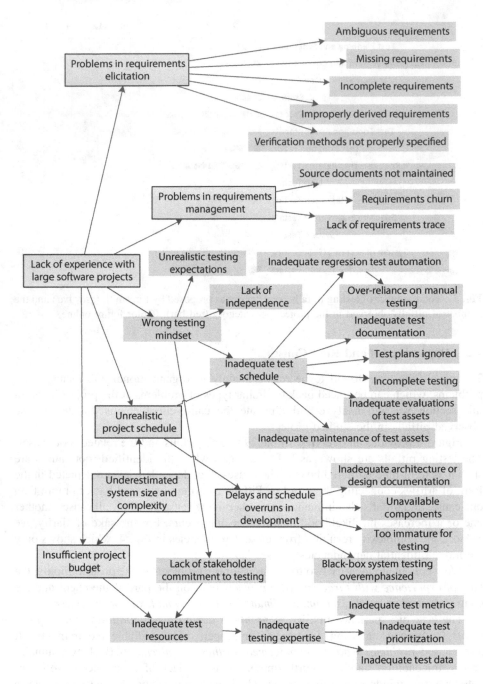

Fig. 4. Observed testing pitfalls (red boxes) traced back to root causes (blue bordered boxes). (Color figure online)

suffered from *delays and schedule overruns*. Components were released too late, not properly unit tested and documented, and thus they were often still too immature for the later integration and system testing phases. Due to the inadequate testing schedule, the guidelines defined in the original test plan were mainly ignored. Many test cases were not reviewed or systematically maintained. Test runs were often incomplete and not properly documented. Also, there was not enough time to automate the regression tests which led to an over-reliance on manual testing.

Lastly, the two root causes led to *insufficient project budget* with the effect that not enough testers with adequate expertise were available. Due to this lack of expertise, inadequate test metrics and test data were used, and test cases were not prioritized.

4.3 Additional Project-Specific Pitfalls

Besides the testing pitfalls listed in Firesmith's book [10], we identified several additional issues when we analyzed the problems in the studied project. The following issues had a considerable negative impact on how testing was performed.

Due to the lack of experience, the role of a quality manager was not foreseen in the project plan. Thus, there were no common guidelines for specification and documentation. The testers were the only ones responsible for ensuring the quality. The wrong mindset regarding quality and testing also led to an overreliance on testing, expecting that quality will be "tested into" the system rather than understanding that quality has to be established as part of all engineering and management activities.

Continuing difficulties emerged from the limited mutual understanding of testers and developers. The testers did not have adequate training, experience, and expertise in the smart metering domain, which negatively affected the efficiency and quality of the testing activities and the communication with developers. The developers did not consider testability as an important aspect when implementing the software, thus making the job unnecessarily hard for the testers. In particular, testability issues were found to hinder the automation of the tests.

Problems in test automation were worsened because stakeholders mistakenly believed that typical testers will also be good test automation engineers. When the original test team was replaced by new staff, there was no one left who had any experience with test automation. In the end, an automation specialist from abroad was called in, who had the required skills but did not speak the official project language.

These issues may not be as common as the pitfalls described in Firesmith's book. However, in his recent work [13], Firesmith presented an extended list of potential candidates for common pitfalls that have not yet been included in the catalogue. We mapped the additionally identified issues to the candidate pitfalls (Table 2), suggesting that they may be incorporated in a future edition of the pitfall catalogue.

4.4 Comparison to Related Work

There are only a few studies investigating concrete practical issues and real-world problems in software testing based on challenged or failed projects. In this section we identify studies closely related to our work and we compare the findings reported in these studies to the findings we derived from the analyzed smart metering project.

Table 2. Additional candidates for common pitfalls [13] encountered in the studied project.

Staffing pitfalls	
(a) Testers responsible for ensuring quality	Testers are (solely) responsible for the quality of the system or software under test
(b) Inadequate domain expertise	Testers do not have adequate training, experience, and expertise in the system's application domain
Test process pitfalls	
(c) Testing in quality	Testing stakeholders rely on testing quality into the system/software rather than building quality in from the beginning
(d) Developers ignore testability	The system or software under test (SUT) is unnecessarily difficult to test because the developers did not consider testing when designing and implementing the system or software
Automated testing pitfalls	
(d) Testers make good test automation engineers	It is mistakenly believed that typical testers will be good test automation engineers

Martin, Rooksby, Rouncefield, and Sommerville conducted an ethnographic study on "bad" software testing in a small, agile company [8]. They identified "good" reasons that justified the way software testing was performed in the studied setting. Problems in testing were a result of organizational and commercial pressures for rapid delivery of results, which required coping with limited resources and timeframes. The practical challenge in testing was to demonstrate that software is "good enough" with minimal effort and time. Suggested improvements to testing are less technical in nature but tied to organizational and inter-organizational means. Based on their findings, they conducted a further study investigating the social and organizational dimensions in four projects [14], which confirmed that there is congruence between organizational structure, organizational priorities and the way testing is performed. Hence, they concluded that the problem of improving software testing should be primarily seen as a socio-technical challenge. Their findings closely match the insights we gained when we traced the problems in testing back to management issues in the overall project.

Kasurinen, Taipale and Smolander explored the problems of software testing in real world with the goal to better understand the complex practice of software testing and to find improvement proposals for identified issues. They conducted a survey of testing practices, interviewed practitioners from 26 organizations, and analyzed testing problems in an in-depth grounded theory case study with five selected organizations [15]. They developed seven categories to describe the common themes of test process observations: testing tools, testing automation, knowledge transfer between stakeholders, product design, testing strategy and planning, testing personnel, and testing resources. These categories strongly overlap with the categories used in our paper. Furthermore, they used these categories to identify factors that affect the testing process. In [9] they illustrated the relations between the most essential factors using a cause-effect graph, identifying following top-level factors: business orientation, stability of testing schedules, complexity of testing, and use of components in software testing. Again, there are strong parallels between their findings and the root causes we identified, which further confirms the results we obtained in our investigation. In contrast to their work, we started with a much more comprehensive list of pitfalls and, thus, we were able to draw a more detailed picture of causes and effects.

The comparison of the work presented in this paper with related work also revealed that software testing research is often based on the assumption that the practical constraints inherited from the overall project context are valid and justified. Hence, software testing has to accept these constraints and adapt to them for the greater good of an economically and organizationally balanced project setting. Yet, our insights show that such assumptions need to be questioned. In the studied project, many of the challenges encountered in software testing were caused by mistakes and shortcomings on the project level. The underestimated effort for implementing the overall system, for example, forced testing into an unrealistic schedule with several negative consequences such as an over-reliance on manual testing and the inadequate maintenance of test assets. Reducing testing to its core tasks may help to reach short-term goals and budgetary targets, but this "optimization" caused delays in later steps and led to unnecessary extra costs for rework on the long run.

4.5 Threats to Validity

Our experience report is based on observations made about testing activities embedded in context of a larger software systems engineering project. Since our results and findings are derived from a single project, their generalization (external validity) may be limited. Even though we consider the studied project as a representative instance of a large, critical project with multiple stakeholders, there may not be another project with the exact same characteristics. Nevertheless, the insights we draw from our observations can still be relevant for a broader set of projects that are conducted in a similar setting. By analyzing the project through the lens of commonly observed testing pitfalls, we aim at further improving external validity.

The main point in relying on a comprehensive and documented catalogue of commonly observed pitfalls was to improve construct validity and internal validity. The pitfalls as well as their potential consequences and causes are described in the book by Firesmith [10]. This book provides a solid basis for our work and a way to triangulate the previous observations and insights about testing in the analyzed project, which were obtained from consulting and review activities over several years.

The specific role of the authors and the prolonged involvement of one of the authors in the studied project pose, on the one hand, a further potential threat to validity but, on the other hand, also provide the benefit of having detailed, first-hand knowledge resulting from personally participating in meetings and key decisions, consulting with different members of the project team, and performing reviews of specifications, design documents, test plans, etc. In that sense, data acquisition involved several different sources, even though the data was not collected with the objective of conducting a scientific study.

5 Conclusions

In this paper we described the problems in software and system testing identified in a large and complex real-world project on developing a smart metering system. We compared these problems with a catalogue of commonly encountered testing pitfalls and traced them back to their root causes at the overall project level. We found that the majority of the identified problems are not new or specific to the studied project as they are closely related to documented pitfalls that have been observed in multiple other projects before. Still, the project has repeatedly fallen into these pitfalls due to several mistakes made by managers, requirements engineers, and testers throughout all project phases. The two main causes we identified as the root of most of the observed problems were the lack of experience with large software projects and the underestimated size and complexity of the system.

Based on our observations and findings, we identified a number of lessons learned and suggestions on how to mitigate the identified problems and on how to improve software testing practice in general.

- *Treat common pitfalls as risks.* Review the catalogue of commonly observed pitfalls and identify potential pitfalls as risks, which should be added to the project's risk repository to be managed accordingly.
- *Conduct project and test process reviews* in order to make sure that existing pitfalls are identified and diagnosed early, when there is still time for applying counter-measures and corrective actions.
- *Provide training on software testing and test management* also for personnel outside the testing team such as acquisition staff, project managers, and requirements engineers to create awareness about testing pitfalls and how to prevent them.
- *Perform adequate requirements engineering.* Plan enough time and resources for requirements definition and management because poor requirements will inevitably result in testing problems and, ultimately, in costly extra work of resolving quality problems and fixing the flawed system.
- *Realistic estimation and planning of testing time and effort.* Estimates require the involvement of knowledgeable and experienced testers. Furthermore, estimates should be made independent from the project's budget and time constraints. Aligning the estimates to the constraints and vice versa is achieved by planning.
- *Acquire necessary know-how and support when needed.* When lacking the required experience in one or more areas, avoid falling into common pitfalls due to "learning by doing" but seek support from professional consultants.
- *Treat testing and test automation as an investment decision.* Testing and, in particular, the automation of testing should not be driven by technical considerations. Analyze early on which test automation approach is best suited for the project from an economical perspective. Model-based generation of test scripts, for instance, can help to ensure sustained efficiency and maintainability [16] leading to a significant return on investment for a project.

Under the light of our findings, one has to reconsider what research can actually help to improve the situation of software testing in practice. As long as projects are stuck in the same commonly known testing pitfalls, there is little chance for research to have an impact. Hence, our plans for future work focus on the development of measures for the early recognition of common pitfalls in software and system testing and ways for communicating them.

Acknowledgments. This research has been supported by the Austrian Research Pro-motion Agency, the Austrian Ministry for Transport, Innovation and Technology, the Federal Ministry of Science, Research and Economy, and the Province of Upper Austria in the frame of the COMET center SCCH (FFG 844597).

References

1. Tricentis: Software Fail Watch, 5th Ed. White paper, 27 February 2018, Tricentis (2018). https://www.tricentis.com/software-fail-watch/. Accessed 25 Aug 2018
2. ISO/IEC/IEEE: International Standard 29119-1 Software and systems engineering - Software testing - Part 1: Concepts and definitions. Institute of Electrical and Electronics Engineers (2013)
3. Jones, C., Bonsignour, O.: The Economics of Software Quality. Addison-Wesley Professional, Upper Saddle River (2011)
4. Bertolino, A.: Software testing research: achievements, challenges, dreams. In: Future of Software Engineering. IEEE Computer Society (2007)
5. Orso, A., Rothermel, G.: Software testing: a research travelogue (2000–2014). In: Proceedings of the on Future of Software Engineering. ACM (2014)
6. Scargle, J.D.: Publication bias: the "File-Drawer" problem in scientific inference. J. Sci. Explor. **14**(1), 91–106 (2000)
7. Tassey, G.: The economic impacts of inadequate infrastructure for software testing. National Institute of Standards and Technology, RTI Project, 7007-011 (2002)
8. Martin, D., Rooksby, J., Rouncefield, M., Sommerville, I.: 'Good' organisational reasons for 'Bad' software testing: an ethnographic study of testing in a small software company. In: Proceedings of the 29th International Conference on Software Engineering. IEEE Computer Society (2007)
9. Kasurinen, J., Taipale, O., Smolander, K.: Analysis of problems in testing practices. In: Proceedings of the 2009 Asia-Pacific Software Engineering Conference, APSEC 2009. IEEE (2009)
10. Firesmith, D.: Common System and Software Testing Pitfalls: How to Prevent and Mitigate Them: Descriptions, Symptoms, Consequences, Causes, and Recommendations. Addison Wesley Professional, Upper Saddle River (2013)
11. European Commission: Mandate M/441 - Standardisation mandate to CEN, CENELEC and ETSI in the field of measuring instruments for the development of an open architecture for utility meters involving communication protocols enabling interoperability. European Commission, Enterprise and Industry Directorate-General, M/441 EN (2009)
12. Elsberg, M.: Blackout: Tomorrow Will Be Too Late. Penguin Books, London (2017)
13. Firesmith, D.G.: Common system and software testing pitfalls. In: Proceedings of the Team Software Process Symposium 2014 (TSP-2014), Pittsburgh, Pennsylvania. SEI (2014). https://resources.sei.cmu.edu/library/asset-view.cfm?assetID=423692
14. Rooksby, J., Rouncefield, M., Sommerville, I.: Testing in the wild: the social and organisational dimensions of real world practice. Comput. Support. Coop. Work (CSCW) **18**(5–6), 559–580 (2009)

15. Taipale, O., Smolander, K.: Improving software testing by observing practice. In: Proceedings of the 2006 ACM/IEEE International Symposium on Empirical Software Engineering. ACM (2006)
16. Mohacsi, S., Felderer, M., Beer, A.: Estimating the cost and benefit of model-based testing: a decision support procedure for the application of model-based testing in industry. In: Proceedings of the Euromicro SEAA, Madeira, Portugal (2015)

Knowledge Engineering and Machine Learning

Mixed Reality Applications in Industry: Challenges and Research Areas

Thomas Moser[3]($\boxtimes$), Markus Hohlagschwandtner[1], Gerhard Kormann-Hainzl[2], Sabine Pölzlbauer[1], and Josef Wolfartsberger[4]

[1] FOTEC Forschungs- und Technologietransfer GmbH, Wiener Neustadt, Austria
{hohlagschwandtner,poelzlbauer}@fotec.at
[2] IMC University of Applied Sciences Krems, Krems, Austria
gerhard.kormann@fh-krems.ac.at
[3] St. Pölten University of Applied Sciences, St. Pölten, Austria
thomas.moser@fhstp.ac.at
[4] University of Applied Sciences Upper Austria, Campus Steyr, Steyr, Austria
josef.wolfartsberger@fh-steyr.at

Abstract. Mixed reality (both virtual reality and augmented reality) technologies and applications have become increasingly important in recent years. However, from a technical, organizational and psychological point of view, there are still some challenges for industrial use in real operation - this is also proven by the well-known hype cycle of Gartner, who currently sees the technology in the 'valley of disappointment'. The currently available products in the field of mixed reality are to be considered as individual solutions throughout and also suitable for a wide application under industrial conditions only conditionally. In addition, pre-projects with production companies and plant manufacturers show that the technologies and the associated operational opportunities are still largely unexploited for SMEs. This paper summarizes the challenges and potential research fields in the areas of interaction and usability, immersion and storytelling, and international business processes and stakeholder acceptance.

Keywords: Mixed reality · Industrial applications · Interaction Immersion · Storytelling · Stakeholder acceptance

1 Introduction

Mixed reality technologies and applications have become increasingly important in recent years. Mixed Reality (MR) describes technologies between completely real environment and completely virtual environment [23]. The two most prominent representatives within the Mixed Reality Continuum (also known as Reality Virtuality Continuum), which stretches between the real and fully virtual environments, are Virtual Reality or Virtual Reality (VR) and Augmented Reality or Augmented Reality (AR) (see Fig. 1).

© Springer Nature Switzerland AG 2019
D. Winkler et al. (Eds.): SWQD 2019, LNBIP 338, pp. 95–105, 2019.
https://doi.org/10.1007/978-3-030-05767-1_7

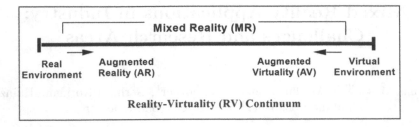

Fig. 1. The mixed reality continuum as defined by Paul Milgram [23].

Many important players in the IT environment are pushing into the MR market. Examples include Microsoft HoloLens, Google (Daydream, Cardboard, Tango, ARCore), Facebook (Oculus Rift), Sony (PlayStation VR), Valve/HTC (HTC Vive) [2]. Over the past few months, companies such as Apple (ARKit), Acer, Asus, Dell, HP and Lenovo have joined the pack of vendors. The goal of MR is to stimulate the user's senses in such a way that the real and digital world merge into a believable whole. The focus is on integrating additional information in the user's field of vision [3]. The technical challenge lies in the exact registration of virtual and real content. MR (and also VR) requires the representation of computer-generated 3D graphics in real time and often accesses new types of hardware. In the VR environment, the rapid development and spread of head-mounted displays (HMDs) and various input devices has been observed in recent years; MR is currently working on improving tracking methods, mostly for mobile devices.

The steady increase in the quality of mixed reality applications and the parallel increase in hardware performance are leading to sustainable acceptance of the technology. Especially for industrial applications, this results in interesting and sustainable application areas for companies, for example for remote support, interactive training and training scenarios, virtual prototyping, design evaluation and support for virtual commissioning. However, current solutions for the industry are still in an experimental stage and often have - especially for professional use absolutely necessary - quite low user acceptance and too low robustness for daily operation. Sustainable use lacks exemplary and successful MR applications and enterprise support in translating knowledge into innovation.

Recent publications and research projects show a clear trend among companies and public institutions towards opening towards collaborative innovation, according to a study by Simon Richir, Université de Lorraine [12]. Immersive and Collaborative Environments (ICEs) based on augmented or mixed reality would be the right way to evaluate innovative ideas and concepts. However, there is a need to design appropriate methods and tools, which would be more advanced than the tools. For example, three different approaches are suggested in the field of methodology: physical implementation, presentation of the result and the way in which results and parameters are evaluated.

These three approaches can be found in countless research projects (Journal of Virtual Reality Society, Journal of Virtual Reality Research, Development and Application Virtual Prototyping Journal). So also many institutes and research institutions deal with result presentation and evaluation:

- Markerless 3D Interaction in an Unconstrained Handheld Mixed Reality Setup [14]
- An Agent-Aware Computing Based Mixed Reality Information System [22]
- Effects of Interaction Level, Framerate, Field of View, 3D Content Feedback, Previous Experience on Subjective User eXperience and Objective Usability in Immersive Virtual Environment [33]
- Empty Room, how to compose and spatialize electroacoustic music in VR in ambisonic and binaural [34].

Physical implementation considerations are primarily implemented by hardware manufacturers and the gaming industry, with little information known to the state of the art (time to market). Also in the area academic research, there are few indications:

- Worm Selector: Volume Selection in a 3D Point Cloud Through Adaptive Modelling [11].

The following sections summarize the challenges and potential research fields in the areas of interaction and usability, immersion and storytelling, and international business processes and stakeholder acceptance. Finally, the last section concludes and identifies field for further research possibilities.

2   Interaction and Usability

Methods for entering and interacting with virtual information in MR systems are critical to its successful use. Billinghurst et al. divide the types of interaction interfaces into information browsers, 3D User Interfaces (3DUI), Tangible User Interfaces (TUI), Natural User Interfaces (NUI), and Multimodal Interfaces [5].

Information browsers are the simplest type of interaction, in which only the spatial orientation of the device makes the information located in the MR visible. Selection and manipulation of the data is usually kept simple and can be realized using traditional interaction devices (mouse, keyboard, etc.). Information browsers are an important category because they are easy to learn because of their reference to traditional input methods. 3D user interfaces allow interaction with virtual objects via controllers, which are used for navigation, selection and manipulation of 3D information [21], above all selection and manipulation in the MR context are the most important. Missing haptic feedback of the virtual objects is often simulated with vibration of the sensors.

Tangible user interfaces often have the problem that there is a local separation between the virtual object being manipulated and the physical input device. Kato et al. describe the concept of Tangible AR (TAR), which expands a physical tangible with visualized virtual information [18]. While TARs have the advantage of an intuitive application, the presence of a physical object for interaction may well be detrimental to mobile or wearable MR applications [5]. For Natural User Interfaces those interaction methods are counted, which allow a manipulation by body and hand gestures, facial expressions, speech recognition, etc. These modalities were made possible by tremendous advances in the classification accuracy of machine learning algorithms to detect, as well as the price decay and commercialization of specialized sensors such as depth cameras, which is why they are already successfully used in marketed systems such as the Microsoft HoloLens. Many studies show that the multimodal application of several previously mentioned methods can significantly increase the speed and precision in performing tasks [5], as the modalities are complementary in terms of their quantitative and qualitative characteristics. Often, the combination of hand gestures with voice input is seen as advantageous.

Remote Support (also known as 'Maintenance 4.0') is one of the most promising mixed reality applications in this context. The employee is guided through the service or maintenance order by means of smart glasses and gets work instructions projected directly into the field of view. In addition, the camera image of the device can be transmitted to a geographically distant expert, who can expand the field of view of the worker purposefully with digital information. Supported by hardware such as HoloLens, local technicians can use real-time, real-time data from a given facility to assess location, and also anchor complementary information at well-defined locations in the facility. This facilitates the day-to-day work of technicians, who can also call up exact instructions for their activities, as required. Changing a filter or building a machine. In addition, the use of the glasses allows the hands remain free. This is expected to result in a significant increase in efficiency for service and maintenance. A German consultancy study[1] found that *more than 60% of production costs are influenced directly and indirectly by the efficiency of maintenance services*. Employees have to be trained for the respective tasks in order to process orders quickly and above all without errors In practice, training on the machine is often too time-consuming or too dangerous (on the fly) MR provides a way to provide the worker with context-sensitive assistance to complete the job quickly and efficiently The interactive nature of MR assisted assistance leads to a sustainable advantage that can significantly reduce the costs of service and maintenance.

3   Immersion and Storytelling

Mixed reality makes it possible to rethink immersive storytelling. Researchers have established the concept of digital storytelling at the latest since the millennium as an important topic [7,16,20,24]. Since 2008, the International Conference on Interactive Digital Storytelling (ICIDS 2001–2007) and the International Conference on Interactive Storytelling and Entertainment (TIDESE

---

[1] https://goo.gl/Jwe7kN.

2003–2006) have formed a cross-disciplinary platform with numerous publications as the International Conference on Interactive Digital Storytelling (ICIDS) [4,15,25,27,31]. The workshop series Computational Models of Narrative (CMN), interlaced as an interdisciplinary event Computer Science as well as other disciplines such as the Association for the Advancement of Artificial Intelligence (AAAI).

As already seen, for the study of storytelling in conjunction with MR, the notions of interactivity and immersion play significant roles [8,10,28,29]. MR systems use interfaces that act as intuitive interfaces between the MR environment and users: '*The human interacts with elements of this task by looking, holding, manipulating, speaking, listening and moving, using as many of their natural skills as are appropriate [...]*' [32]. The natural interaction is counteracted by a 'magical' interaction that, for example, allows teleportation through space [10]. The immersive character of MR often differentiates between technological-physiological immersion and psychological-mental immersion [30]. Marie-Laure Ryan distinguishes between a ludic immersion, such as immersion in a task or game, and narrative immersion, the construction and consideration of a story-world [29]. In the course of an immersive narrative for VR productions, John Bucher [6] is modifying already established dramaturgies with interactive elements: while the Interactive Three-Act Structure and the Interactive Five-Act Structure follow more linear storylines, the Interactive Beat-Based Structure is oriented already on web and gaming formats. Ryan merges mental immersion with VR and interactive storytelling into spatial, temporal and emotional categories to form a 'Poetics of Immersion': '*spatial immersion, the reponse to setting; temporal immersion, the response to story; and emotional immersion, the response to characters*' [29]. The poetics of interactive dramaturgy are also exemplified in a typology: Interactivity and the Epic Plot, the Epistemic Plot, the Dramatic Plot and the Soap Opera Plot. The aforementioned approaches and further typologies form the starting point for the extension of immersive storytelling investigated in the use cases.

As a pioneering technology, Mixed Reality not only offers future-oriented interfaces between industrial application and research, but also to redevelop and implement innovative ways of storytelling in the economy.

4 International Business Processes and Stakeholder Acceptance

Two preliminary studies analyzed the influence of digital technologies, especially MR on international business processes, and tested research designs [19]. A preliminary study has already looked at various types of remote support and their impact on internationalization mode. Based on a literature review on maintenance strategies, an allocation of maintenance strategies to each of the maintenance areas was made as listed in Table 1.

Development in the maintenance area is characterized by a development from reactive to preventive maintenance and finally to preventive maintenance (condition-based maintenance). Traditionally, maintenance services required on-site solutions provided either by the company's own engineers or subcontractors. In the international business environment, there is already a trend toward predictive maintenance based on remote solutions and e-maintenance. Table 1 summarizes each maintenance area, followed by the appropriate service strategies.

Table 1. Maintenance areas and service strategies.

On-Site maintenance	Corrective strategy	Characterized by ad hoc service operations following incidents
	Preventive strategy	Planned maintenance on site
Remote maintenance	Corrective strategy	Ad hoc remote control (with or without on-site action)
	Preventive strategy	Remote-based notification of errors before a failure arises
e-Maintenance	Corrective strategy	Ad hoc internet-based control (with or without on-site action)
	Preventive strategy	Remote-based notification of errors before a failure arises

Concerning the impact on internationalization mode, the Uppsala model for internationalization was analyzed for maintenance service strategies. The Uppsala model raises the following question: what impact does digital transformation-based servitization have on businesses' ongoing activities and market commitment? The preliminary study served as the basis for further research within the scope of the research field.

Within the framework of analyzing stakeholder acceptance, a widespread model of acceptance or its derivatives is used. The Theory of Planned Behavior (TPB) [1] is able to explain more rational decisions or behaviors that occur primarily in business and everyday work.

According to the theory, planned human behavior is guided by three types of considerations: (1) assumptions about the likely outcomes of the behavior and assessments of these results (behavioral beliefs), (2) assumptions about others' normative expectations and motivation, those expectations to meet (normative assumptions/normative beliefs) and assumptions about how much one can control the behavior (control beliefs) or make it easier or more difficult. Subsequently, behavioral assumptions create a positive or negative attitude towards behavior; normative beliefs lead to a perceived social pressure or a subjective norm; and control beliefs lead to perceived behavioral control. The attitude towards behavior, the subjective norm and the perception of behavioral control then together lead to the formation of a behavioral intention. In general, the more positive the attitudes and subjective norms and the greater the perceived control, the stronger the intention of the person should be to perform that behavior. In particular, it is important that as soon as a factor is very bad, it acts as a bottleneck and prevents or reduces the intentions. Finally, people are expected to realize their intentions when the opportunity arises, as they have a sufficient degree of actual control over the behavior. Intention is thus assumed as an immediate prelude to behavior. However, because many behaviors involve difficulty in executing (the 'hands on experience') that can limit the will control, it makes sense to consider a perceived behavioral control in addition to the intent. As the perceived behavioral control becomes generalizable, it can act as a proxy for actual control and predict the behavior.

The Technology Acceptance Model (TAM), developed by Davis [9], is one of the most popular research models for predicting the use and acceptance of individual technologies in different information system constructs.

The TAM is based on the TPB and focuses on two very important factors, the first is perceived usefulness and the second is perceived ease of use. These two factors are very important as soon as it comes to the acceptance of new technologies. Davis defines perceived utility as the subjective probability of the future user using a specific application system to improve his or her work or life performance. The perceived ease of use can be defined as the measure in which the prospective user expects the target system to cost no more effort. According to TAM, usability and perceived usefulness are the most important determinants of actual system usage. These two factors are influenced by external variables. The most important external factors that normally manifest themselves are social factors, cultural factors and political factors. Social factors include language, skills, and facilitated conditions. Political factors are mainly the effects of the use of technology in politics and political crises. The setting for use relates to the user's evaluation of whether it is desirable to use a particular information system application. Behavioral intent is the measure of the likelihood of a person or a group of people to use the application fully in accordance with their intention.

While the TPB takes into account the overall context of changes, the use of TAM selectively analyzes the introduction of a specific technology (e.g., mixed reality maintenance applications, new sales tools, etc.) to make conceptual and operational decisions.

5   Summary and Outlook

The question of how the use of MR technologies affects business processes and special international processes impact on the competitiveness of companies is of crucial importance for the evaluation of a business location.

An example of the relevance of this question can be shown in the appendix to the example of remote service:

1. Maintenance processes are very relevant for global manufacturing companies with maintenance needs of their products.
2. A company's internationalization mode decisions are strongly determined by overcoming distance, both geographical and psychological.

3. Maintenance is closely linked to the core product offer of a company and conclusions on the business process and the business model are thus comprehensible.
4. The maintenance services are already undergoing a digital transformation towards 'servitization' [26], providing ready empirical insights into how the level of service digitization drives the choices or revisions, the production location, and the level of control [13].

Especially globally active companies are facing considerable competitive challenges regarding their business models in the digital age as well as site decisions. The basic hypothesis is that MR technologies have a significant positive impact on the attractiveness of the business location, as the technologies systematically reduce costs for international processes and business models (Overcoming distance and thus impact on travel costs, communication costs, etc.). The impact on the environment, energy and resource consumption, especially in the field of remote support, is also directly a research-relevant issue, since the main goals for the use of MR applications are the reduction of costs through travel activities, communication, etc.

From a technical point of view there are still some challenges in the field of mixed reality. This is also proven by the well-known hype cycle of Gartner, who still sees the technology in the 'valley of disappointment'. Currently available Mixed Reality products are prototypes. At the beginning of the project, currently available smart glasses should be purchased. However, the risk is high that these devices will still be considered technically obsolete during the project period. In addition, current devices usually can not be tested before and the manufacturers give little price over performance and user acceptance. A well-known example of this is the company Magic Leap, which promises a novel generation of MR-enabled smart glasses. However, little is known about features and hardware specifications. Linked to this is the fact that it is impossible to estimate whether the devices will work in an industrial environment and comply with ergonomic and safety standards at all. Therefore, there is an increased and unpredictable risk in the acceptance of the technology by end users.

Another risk concerns the need for real-time representation of complex data. Throughout the MR environment, data must be output in real time at refresh rates of about 60 fps to quickly adjust the perspective view to the display position and orientation. The refresh rate depends heavily on the complexity of the virtual content to be displayed. In many cases, the raw data (CAD data, scan records, simulation results) from industry and research are too complex to be displayed in real time. This is currently playing an even greater role, as many MR systems are mobile systems with limited battery capacity and limited computing power.

The efficient interaction with scene data records poses another risk. Unlike desktop systems for which keyboard and mouse are standard inputs, and mobile devices that interact with finger touch, input devices are by no means standardized in MR technologies. Here one works with most different, often prototypical input devices as well as gestures or speech recognition. Independent of the lack of established and proven standard input devices and methods, the interaction in three-dimensional space presents another challenge. While de facto standards for the interaction in 2D user interfaces (e.g. selection, manipulation) could not be established for 3D data so that many different and inconsistent solutions coexist. Due to the mobile nature and the lack of external tracking systems, MR mainly works with speech recognition and gesture control. Speech recognition is difficult to use in many application scenarios, undesirable or unrealizable due to the environmental level (especially in the industrial context). Gestures can often be used for interaction, for example to implement simple operations, such as the selection of menu items. If complex text input or precise positioning of virtual objects in the room is required, gesture control is not ideal. Two other major gestures in the room are the lack of tactile feedback and fatigue of the user's arms [17]. In sum, this poses a high risk for the acceptance of the technology.

References

1. Ajzen, I.: The theory of planned behavior. Organ. Behav. Hum. Decis. Process. **50**(2), 179–211 (1991). https://doi.org/10.1016/0749-5978(91)90020-T. http://linkinghub.elsevier.com/retrieve/pii/074959789190020T
2. Anthes, C., Garcia-Hernandez, R.J., Wiedemann, M., Kranzlmuller, D.: State of the art of virtual reality technology. In: 2016 IEEE Aerospace Conference, pp. 1–19. IEEE, March 2016. https://doi.org/10.1109/AERO.2016.7500674. http://ieeexplore.ieee.org/document/7500674/
3. Azuma, R.T.: A survey of augmented reality. Presence Teleoperators Virtual Environ. **6**(4), 355–385 (1997). https://doi.org/10.1162/pres.1997.6.4.355. http://www.mitpressjournals.org/doi/10.1162/pres.1997.6.4.355
4. Balet, O., Subsol, G., Torguet, P. (eds.): Virtual Storytelling. Using Virtual Reality Technologies for Storytelling. Lecture Notes in Computer Science, vol. 2897. Springer, Heidelberg (2003). https://doi.org/10.1007/b94275. http://link.springer.com/10.1007/b94275
5. Billinghurst, M., Clark, A., Lee, G.: A survey of augmented reality. Found. Trends® Hum. Comput. Interact. **8**(2), 73–272 (2015). https://doi.org/10.1561/1100000049. http://www.nowpublishers.com/article/Details/HCI-049
6. Bucher, J.: Storytelling for Virtual Reality. Taylor and Francis, New York (2017). http://www.myilibrary.com?id=1020285. OCLC: 993684097
7. Crawford, C.: Chris Crawford on Interactive Storytelling, 2nd edn. New Riders, Berkeley (2013)
8. Cruz-Neira, C., Sandin, D.J., DeFanti, T.A.: Surround-screen projection-based virtual reality: the design and implementation of the CAVE. In: Proceedings of the 20th Annual Conference on Computer Graphics and Interactive Techniques, SIGGRAPH 1993, pp. 135–142. ACM Press (1993). https://doi.org/10.1145/166117.166134. http://portal.acm.org/citation.cfm?doid=166117.166134
9. Davis, F.D.: A technology acceptance model for empirically testing new end-user information systems: theory and results (1985)
10. Dörner, R., Broll, W., Grimm, P., Jung, B. (eds.): Virtual und Augmented Reality (VR/AR). eXamen.press, Springer, Heidelberg (2013). https://doi.org/10.1007/978-3-642-28903-3. http://link.springer.com/10.1007/978-3-642-28903-3
11. Dubois, E., Hamelin, A.: Worm selector: volume selection in a 3d point cloud through adaptive modelling. Int. J. Virtual Reality (IJVR) **17**(1), 1–20 (2017). https://hal.archives-ouvertes.fr/hal-01530735

12. Dupont, L., Pallot, M., Morel, L., Christmann, O., Boly, V., Simon Richir, P.: Exploring mixed-methods instruments for performance evaluation of immersive collaborative environments. Int. J. Virtual Reality (IJVR) **17**(2), 1–29 (2017). https://hal.archives-ouvertes.fr/hal-01634942

13. Ekeledo, I., Sivakumar, K.: The impact of e-commerce on entry-mode strategies of service firms: a conceptual framework and research propositions. J. Int. Mark. **12**(4), 46–70 (2004). https://doi.org/10.1509/jimk.12.4.46.53212. http://journals.ama.org/doi/abs/10.1509/jimk.12.4.46.53212

14. Fritz, D., Mossel, A., Kaufmann, H.: Markerless 3d interaction in an unconstrained handheld mixed reality setup. Int. J. Virtual Reality (IJVR) **15**(1), 25–34 (2015). https://hal.archives-ouvertes.fr/hal-01530620

15. Göbel, S., et al. (eds.): Technologies for Interactive Digital Storytelling and Entertainment. Lecture Notes in Computer Science, vol. 3105. Springer, Heidelberg (2004). https://doi.org/10.1007/b98252. http://link.springer.com/10.1007/b98252

16. Hagebölling, H. (ed.): Interactive Dramaturgies. X.media.publishing, Springer, Heidelberg (2004). https://doi.org/10.1007/978-3-642-18663-9. http://link.springer.com/10.1007/978-3-642-18663-9

17. Hincapié-Ramos, J.D., Guo, X., Moghadasian, P., Irani, P.: Consumed endurance: a metric to quantify arm fatigue of mid-air interactions. In: Proceedings of the SIGCHI Conference on Human Factors in Computing Systems, CHI 2014, pp. 1063–1072. ACM (2014). http://doi.acm.org/10.1145/2556288.2557130

18. Kato, H., Billinghurst, M., Poupyrev, I., Imamoto, K., Tachibana, K.: Virtual object manipulation on a table-top AR environment. In: Proceedings IEEE and ACM International Symposium on Augmented Reality (ISAR 2000), pp. 111–119. IEEE (2000). https://doi.org/10.1109/ISAR.2000.880934. http://ieeexplore.ieee.org/document/880934/

19. Kormann, G., Andersson, S., Moser, R., Wictor, I.: Will the digital transformation become a game changer in the field of internationalisation research? In: International Entrepreneurship in a Multi-Speed Global Economy: Opportunities and Challenges. University of Economics and Business, Wien (2015). http://www.bbk.ac.uk/management/about-us/events/mie-conference/mcgill.pdf

20. Lambert, J.: Digital Storytelling: Capturing Lives, Creating Community, 4th edn. Routledge, London (2013)

21. LaViola, J.J., Kruijff, E., McMahan, R.P., Bowman, D.A., Poupyrev, I.: 3D user Interfaces: Theory and Practice. Addison-Wesley Usability and HCI Series, 2nd edn. Addison-Wesley, Redwood City (2017). OCLC: ocn935986831

22. Liu, C.Z., Kavakli, M.: An agent-aware computing based mixed reality information system. Int. J. Virtual Reality **17**(3) (2017)

23. Milgram, P., Takemura, H., Utsumi, A., Kishino, F.: Augmented reality: a class of displays on the reality-virtuality continuum. In: Das, H. (ed.) Telemanipulator and Telepresence Technologies, pp. 282–292. SPIE, December 1995. https://doi.org/10.1117/12.197321. http://proceedings.spiedigitallibrary.org/proceeding.aspx?articleid=981543

24. Miller, C.H.: Digital Storytelling: A Creator's Guide to Interactive Entertainment, 2nd edn. Focal Press/Elsevier, Amsterdam (2008). OCLC: ocn182553069

25. Mitchell, A., Fernández-Vara, C., Thue, D. (eds.): Interactive Storytelling. Lecture Notes in Computer Science, vol. 8832. Springer, Heidelberg (2014). https://doi.org/10.1007/978-3-319-12337-0. http://link.springer.com/10.1007/978-3-319-12337-0

26. Muller, A., Crespo Marquez, A., Iung, B.: On the concept of e-maintenance: review and current research. Reliab. Eng. Syst. Saf. **93**(8), 1165–1187 (2008). https://doi.org/10.1016/j.ress.2007.08.006. http://linkinghub.elsevier.com/retrieve/pii/S0951832007002189

27. Nack, F., Gordon, A.S. (eds.): Interactive Storytelling. Lecture Notes in Computer Science, vol. 10045. Springer, Heidelberg (2016). https://doi.org/10.1007/978-3-319-48279-8. http://link.springer.com/10.1007/978-3-319-48279-8

28. Pimentel, K., Teixeira, K.: Virtual Reality: Through the New Looking Glass, 1st edn. Intel/Windcrest, New York (1993)

29. Ryan, M.L.: Narrative as Virtual Reality 2: Revisiting Immersion and Interactivity in Literature and Electronic Media, 2nd edn. Johns Hopkins University Press, Baltimore (2015)

30. Sadowski, W., Stanney, K.: Presence in virtual environments. Human factors and ergonomics. In: Handbook of Virtual Environments: Design, Implementation, and Applications, pp. 791–806 (2002)

31. Spierling, U., Szilas, N. (eds.): Interactive Storytelling. Lecture Notes in Computer Science, vol. 5334. Springer, Heidelberg (2008). https://doi.org/10.1007/978-3-540-89454-4. http://link.springer.com/10.1007/978-3-540-89454-4

32. Stone, R.J.: Virtual reality: a tool for telepresence and human factors research. In: Virtual Reality Systems, pp. 181–202. Elsevier (1993). https://doi.org/10.1016/B978-0-12-227748-1.50021-4. http://linkinghub.elsevier.com/retrieve/pii/B9780122277481500214

33. Tcha-Tokey, K., Loup-Escande, E., Christmann, O., Richir, S.: Effects of interaction level, framerate, field of view, 3d content feedback, previous experience on subjective user eXperience and objective usability in immersive virtual environment. Int. J. Virtual Reality **17**, 27–51 (2017)

34. Webster, C., Garnier, F., Sedes, A.: Empty room, how to compose and spatialize electroacoustic music in VR in ambisonic and binaural. Int. J. Virtual Reality (IJVR) **17**(2), 30–39 (2017). https://hal.archives-ouvertes.fr/hal-01634943

Improving Defect Localization by Classifying the Affected Asset Using Machine Learning

Sam Halali[1], Miroslaw Staron[1] (ID), Miroslaw Ochodek[1,2](✉) (ID),
and Wilhelm Meding[3]

[1] Chalmers | University of Gothenburg, Gothenburg, Sweden
miroslaw.staron@cse.gu.se
[2] Institute of Computing Science, Poznan University of Technology, Poznań, Poland
miroslaw.ochodek@cs.put.poznan.pl
[3] Ericsson AB, Gothenburg, Sweden
wilhelm.meding@ericsson.com

Abstract. A vital part of a defect's resolution is the task of defect localization. Defect localization is the task of finding the exact location of the defect in the system. The defect report, in particular, the asset attribute, helps the person assigned to handle the problem to limit the search space when investigating the exact location of the defect. However, research has shown that oftentimes reporters initially assign values to these attributes that provide incorrect information. In this paper, we propose and evaluate the way of automatically identifying the location of a defect using machine learning to classify the source asset. By training an Support-Vector-Machine (SVM) classifier with features constructed from both categorical and textual attributes of the defect reports we achieved an accuracy of 58.52% predicting the source asset. However, when we trained an SVM to provide a list of recommendations rather than a single prediction, the recall increased to up to 92.34%. Given these results, we conclude that software development teams can use these algorithms to predict up to ten potential locations, but already with three predicted locations, the teams can get useful results with the accuracy of over 70%.

Keywords: Defect localization · Machine learning · Case study

1 Introduction

Defect discovery and management in modern software development focus on speed and agility, as modern software development organizations strive to increase the customer responsiveness and quality of their products [4,12]. As delivery times become shorter, the need for fast feedback and quick response time for defect management become essential. Continuous integration and continuous deployment are often adopted to address the needs for fast feedback and quick delivery [17].

© Springer Nature Switzerland AG 2019
D. Winkler et al. (Eds.): SWQD 2019, LNBIP 338, pp. 106–122, 2019.
https://doi.org/10.1007/978-3-030-05767-1_8

In order to optimize the speed of defect management, one can use machine learning to assign defects to development teams as has been done by Jonsson et al. [9]. This paper showed the potential of saving quality managers' time by automatically suggesting which teams could be the best to solve given defects. However, once the team gets the defect assigned to it, the team needs to further investigate which components should be debugged in order to find and repair the defect. In this paper, we address the problem of how to automate the process of finding this component. First, we set off to explore which machine learning algorithm is the most suitable for assigning defects to source assets, such as software components or documents. Then, we investigate how to create and optimize the feature vectors[1] used to achieve the best possible accuracy of predictions. Finally, we investigate how to provide the recommendations to the practitioners, in particular whether it is better to provide a recommendation of a single asset (e.g., "there is 50% probability that the defect is located in Module A") or whether it is better to provide the recommendation of multiple artifacts (e.g., "there is 75% probability that the defect is located in Module A, B or C").

As a methodology, we use Design Science Research (DSR) to design an artifact (a classifier) that will support defect reporters by suggesting the source asset from which a defect could originate from. We investigate three strategies to design a classifier that will provide predictions:

- Choice of classification algorithm—as stated by the No Free Lunch Theorem [15] there is no single algorithm that works best for every problem, and therefore we will perform a simulation study to select the classification algorithm that provides the best accuracy of prediction for the considered problem.
- Feature engineering—we will investigate the possibility of extracting different features from the attributes of a defect report and find a set of features that provide the most accurate predictions.
- Converting the classification problem into a recommendation problem—since the original considered problem is a multiclass classification problem with a large number of decision classes, we will investigate the possibilities of simplifying the problem to balance the prediction accuracy and practical usefulness of the provided results.

We conduct our study together with a large infrastructure provider company in Sweden. We study two mature products, which have been on the market for over a decade and has been developed by a large number of developers. The products have a professionally maintained defect database with a high quality of defect descriptions, their history, timeline, and resolutions.

Our results show that a Support-Vector-Machine (SVM) classifier with features constructed from both categorical and textual attributes of the defect reports provide an accuracy of 58.52% for predicting the most probable location of a defect. However, when we trained an SVM to provide a list of recommendations rather than a single prediction, the recall increased to up to 92.34%.

---

[1] A feature is an attribute describing an entity (in our case a defect). A single entity is described as a vector of features.

A useful breakpoint of 70% accuracy is achieved already when providing three locations (out of over 40) as the recommendation.

The rest of the paper is structured as follows. Section 2 presents the most significant related work in this area. Section 3 presents the design of our study. Section 4 details the results of our study. Finally, Sect. 5 concludes the paper and outlines further work in the area of recommending defect locations.

2   Related Work

Previously, no research has been conducted in predicting the asset attribute of a defect report. However, using machine learning for predicting other defect-report attributes and improving the process of defect resolution is not uncommon. In the systematic mapping study conducted by Cavalcanti et al. [5], it was reported that most research on the topic of defect classification is centered on defect assignment and duplicate detection. Furthermore, Cavalcanti et al. noted that previous research could be extended to classify other defect attributes, such as asset and severity, that are recorded manually. This could be helpful for less experienced reporters when reporting a defect.

2.1   Defect Assignment

Automating the task of defect assignment is a well-studied research problem. In a systematic review by Goyal and Sardana [6], 75 papers investigating the problem were reviewed to find that one of the most common approaches to automate defect assignment being machine learning.

Previous studies have evaluated several classification techniques with the most common evaluation metric being accuracy [6]. The reported accuracies of individual classifiers ranged from 25% [3] to 64% [1] with a higher accuracy being reported by with the use of meta-algorithms [8,23]. The most common features were constructed from the descriptions of defect reports using TF-IDF [6]. However, categorical attribute such as *Asset* [1–3,11,23], *Artifact* [1,3], *Submitter* [9,11] and *Detection Activty* [11] were also used.

When evaluating the developed classification model, Banitaan et al. [2] reported that the features constructed from asset attributes were the most influential features for three out of four datasets that were used. Similar findings were reported by Annvik et al. [1] who improved the accuracy of their classification model for Eclipse by 48% when using features constructed from the asset attributes. However, both papers validated the performance of their classification models using resolved defect reports. Therefore, the effect of the asset attribute being assigned an incorrect value was never observed.

2.2   Duplicate Defect Report Detection

A duplicate defect report describes a defect that already has been reported and submitted to a defect tracking system (DTS). Since duplicated entries are obviously not welcomed, organizations often designate some of their staff to investigate the incoming defect reports to look for duplicates [5].

Several methods to automate the process of detecting duplicate defect reports have been proposed utilizing the description of the defect report to measure the similarity between defect reports [7,14,21,22]. By using TF-IDF to construct features from the defect description, Jalbert et al. [7] developed a model that managed to filter out 8% of the duplicate defect reports before they reached the DTS. With a detection rate of 8%, the model could not replace the manual process required for detecting duplicates. However, the model could reduce the number of defect reports to be inspected manually. Since the model's detection rate of non-duplicates was 100%, the only cost of deploying the model would be the cost of classifying each defect report. The time required for classifying a defect report was reported to be 20 s.

Tian et al. [22] developed a classification model with a detection rate of 24% by also including features constructed from the categorical attributes of a defect report. However, the improvement of the detection rate led to a loss of 9% of the non-duplicate detection rate.

2.3   Defect Prediction in Industry

Prediction models in the domain of software defects are widely studied. Most of the conducted studies were related to defects in open source software. However, there were also studies performed in the domain of large-scale software projects in industry, mainly related to Defect Inflow Prediction [18,19] and Software Defect Prediction [13].

Defect Inflow Prediction is the task of predicting the number of non-redundant defects being reported into the DTS [19]. In the study, conducted by Staron et al. [19], a model for predicting the defect inflow during the planning phase for up to 3 weeks in advance was proposed. The model was constructed using multivariate linear regression and modeled the defect inflow as a function of characteristics of work packages. The results showed that the model could support project managers to estimate the work effort needed for completing the project by providing a prediction accuracy of defect inflow of 72%.

To make the testing phase more efficient a software defect prediction (SDP) model can be used. SDP is the task of predicting software assets which are prone to defects. By using the SDP model organizations can make testing more efficient by allocating more resources to the predicted assets [13]. Predicting assets prone to defect can be done using machine learning. Rana et al. [13] highlights that the problem can be either a classification or a regression problem.

A classification model for SDP classifies modules that are represented by software metrics and code attributes as fault-prone or non-fault-prone based on previous projects [10]. For this task, several algorithms including Naive Bayes, Logistic Regression, Decision Trees, Support Vector Machines, Artificial Neural Networks and K-Nearest Neighbors were used and showed promising results. However, the comparative study conducted by Lessmann et al. [10] concluded that the choice of the classification algorithm had little importance when comparing the performance of the 17 most accurate classifiers that were studied.

3   Research Methodology

The aim of this Design Science Research study is to develop an artifact being a model for classifying the asset from which a defect originate using historic defect reports. In particular, we focus on answering the following knowledge questions:

- **RQ 1:** What classification algorithm provides the highest prediction quality for assigning defects to source assets (e.g. components, documents)?
  RQ 2: What set of features extracted from the defect reports allows achieving the best quality of predictions?
- **RQ 3:** How can we balance prediction quality and practical usefulness of the predictions?
  We answer these questions by performing a simulation study on the dataset of defect reports provided by a large infrastructure provider company.

3.1   Dataset

The dataset provided by the company contained defect reports for two of their software products (denoted as Product 1 and Product 2). The reports were submitted by both customers and employees between 2010 and 2018. Both of the products are mature and consist of several million lines of code each. They are also being actively developed by a few hundred developers. The products are deployed internationally and each has more than 10,000 submitted historic defect reports[2].

In this study, we used the defect-report attributes that were mandatory to record by defect reporters to avoid missing data. The mandatory attributes were: *Description, Severity, Detection Activity, Artifact* and *Asset* (see Table 1 for more details).

Defect reports which were not addressed or resolved were removed since they could not have been used during training or validation. This was because the asset attribute of the defect reports could be reassigned during the resolution process. Therefore, the assigned value could be incorrect since the value was not final. Also, the defect reports that described failures which were not caused by a defect were removed. These failures could, for instance, be caused by not following the documentation when configuring the system. Since the reported failure was not caused by a defect, it would not result in a corrective measure in an asset. Therefore, the assigned value of the asset attribute could be considered incorrect.

The number of candidate source assets (decision classes) in the resulting dataset were more than 40 and 100 for Product 1 and Product 2, respectively[3].

---

[2] Since the information about defects is considered as sensitive data, we are not allowed to provide precise information about the size of the dataset.

[3] We are not allowed to provide the exact number of assets since it is a confidential information.

Table 1. The mandatory attributes of the defect reports that were provided by the company.

Attribute	Type	Description
Description	Textual	Description of what is missing, wrong, or unnecessary
Severity	Ordinal	The highest failure impact that the defect could (or did) cause, as determined by (from the perspective of) the organization responsible for software engineering
Detection activity	Nominal	The activity during which the defect was detected (i.e., inspection or testing)
Artifact	Nominal	The specific software work product containing the defect
Asset	Nominal	The software asset (product, component, module, etc.) containing the defect

3.2   Simulation Study Design

We performed a series of simulation studies using different combinations of classification algorithms and feature vectors. We considered both the classical classification problem and its converted version to recommendation problem when the classifier outputs a list of n most probable source assets.

Machine Learning Algorithms. The classification algorithms evaluated for constructing a classification model are presented in Table 2. The set of algorithms was decided based on their use in the related research. As stated by the No Free Lunch Theorem [15] there is no single algorithm that works best for every problem and therefore the most suitable algorithm was decided through the conducted tests. We used the implementation of the algorithms available in the Python *scikit-learn* library [16]. Finally, we decided to exclude neural networks from the comparison due to the long training times and a large number of parameters needed to be tuned.

Feature Engineering. We extracted sets of features from the mandatory defect attributes presented in Table 1. We used the term frequency-inverse document frequency (TF-IDF) to transform textual attribute *Description* to a vector representation of features. The TF-IDF implementation of scikit-learn also offered removal of stop words and tokenizations of words using regular expressions. This was utilized to remove all the stop words defined by Scikit-learn and tokenize the words so that they only contained at least one alphabetical character using the following pattern: $(?ui)\\b\\w*[a-z]+\\w*\b$. The stop words and numerical sequences were removed since they were irrelevant for describing the attribute. The 1000 words which had the highest TF-IDF score were selected since a larger

Table 2. Descriptions of the evaluated classification algorithms.

Classification algorithm	Description
MultinomialNB	Naive Bayes implementation for multinomially distributed data
DecisionTreeClassifier	A decision tree implementation for classification that uses a optimized version of CART
LogisticRegression	A Logistic Regression implementation for classification
KNeighborsClassifier	A K-Nearest Neighbors implementation that uses five neighbors as default
LinearSVC	A SVM for classification that uses a linear kernel with the cost parameter set to 1 as default

number of words would have increased the training time of the model. The categorical attributes of the defect reports were transformed into features by using scikit-learn's algorithm for One-Hot encoding.

Classification Problems. We considered two variants of the classification problem. The first one was a classical multiclass classification problem. It corresponds to the situation when a trained classification model would directly fill the source-asset attribute of the defect report based on other defect-report attributes recorded by the defect reporter (see Fig. 1).

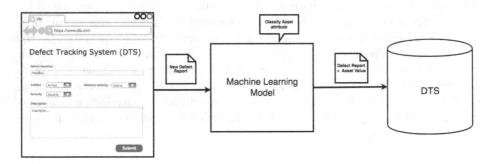

Fig. 1. Classification scheme for the classical variant of the classification problem.

In the second variant, presented in Fig. 2, we consider the situation when the classifier supports the reporter with a list of likely assets for the recorded attributes of the defect report. This would leave the final selection of the source asset to the reporter who would use their expertise to select an asset from the list of recommended assets. Furthermore, the recommendation system could also aid the reporters who have little to no expertise since the list of possible assets would be shortened.

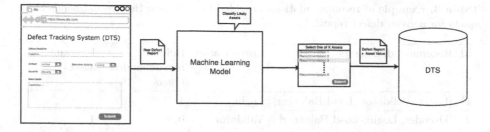

Fig. 2. Classification scheme for the recommendation variant of the problem.

Evaluating Prediction Quality. We used *10-fold cross-validation* with stratified folds as the method for evaluating the prediction accuracy of the models. Stratified folds were used to reduce the variance between the different cross-validation iterations and to maintain the class distribution upon validation.

We performed the simulation runs training each of the classification algorithms presented in Table 2 using three sets of features:

1. learning with features constructed from the categorical attributes,
2. learning with features constructed from the textual attributes,
3. learning with a combination of the features used for the previous tests.

The metrics used for evaluation during the tests for the classical classification problem were *Accuracy, Macro Precision, Macro Recall, Macro F1-Score* and *Matthews Correlation Coefficient*. These metrics allow assessing how a classifier performs across all the decision classes.

We altered the Recall and Precision metrics for the purpose of evaluating the recommendation system variant of the classifier to take into account the fact that the classifier provides a list of source assets as an output. We denote these variants of metrics as *Recall@n* and *Precision@n*.

Recall@n is calculated as the quotient between the number of times the classifier recommended a relevant asset among the n provided assets and all relevant assets among all the recommendations made. Calculating the Recall@3 for the recommendations presented in Table 3 results in a value of approximately 0.667 (66.7%). This is because the number of relevant recommended assets is 2 and the number of relevant assets is 3 across all recommendations.

Similarly, the Precision@n metric would be calculated as the quotient between the number of times the classifier recommended a relevant asset among the n provided assets and the total number of recommended assets. The number of recommended assets used by the Precision@n metric can be simplified to $n \times |relevant\ items|$. Since each defect report only has one correct asset, Recall@n is equivalent to Accuracy. Consequently, Precision@n can be calculated as $Recall@n/n$. When we use the Recall@3 calculated for the recommendations presented in Table 3, we obtain Precision@3 $\approx$ 0.222 (22.2%).

We also trained three simple benchmark classifiers (described in Table 4) as a baseline for the comparisons. These classifiers do not learn anything about

Table 3. Example of recommendations provided by a system that recommends three assets for a given defect report.

Id	Recommended assets	Correct asset	Relevant recommended assets	Relevant assets
1	[Login, Validator, Load Balancer]	Login	1	1
2	[Decoder, Login, Load Balancer]	Validator	0	1
3	[Router, Validator, Decoder]	Router	1	1

the underlying relationships between the features and the target variable but use the class distribution of the training data to assign defects to source assets. If the performance of the classification model did not exceed these benchmarks then it had not gained any knowledge about the functional relationship between the features and the asset and was therefore not considered to be useful by the telecom company.

Table 4. Three benchmark classifiers being used to determine the lower boundaries for prediction quality.

Classifier	Description
Stratified	Classifies entries based on the distribution of the label class in the training set
Most_frequent	Classifies entries based on the most frequent label in the training set
Uniform	Classifies entries uniformly at random

4   Results

4.1   Predicting Single Location

We present the results for the classical classification problem, where we classify each defect into a single decision class being a source asset. We consider three sets of features and report metrics such as macro-Accuracy, averaged *Precision*, *Recall* and *F1-Score*, as well as *MCC*.

Tables 5 and 6 show the performance of the classification models trained with features constructed from the categorical attributes of defect reports from Product 1 and Product 2, respectively. For Product 1, the maximum Accuracy of **26.82%** was achieved by using **LogisticRegression**. For Product 2, the maximum Accuracy of **29.56%** was achieved by using **LinearSVC**.

Tables 7 and 8 show the performance of the classification models trained with features constructed from the textual attributes of defect reports from Product 1 and Product 2, respectively. For Product 1, the maximum Accuracy of **57.36%**

Table 5. Results for models trained with features constructed from the categorical attributes of defect reports from Product 1.

Classifier	Accuracy	Precision (Macro)	Recall (Macro)	F1-score (Macro)	MCC
MultinomialNB	26.28%	7.47%	8.17%	7.29%	0.186
DecisionTreeClassifier	25.93%	8.62%	8.36%	7.88%	0.183
LogisticRegression	**26.82%**	**7.87%**	**8.23%**	**7.31%**	**0.191**
KNeighborsClassifier	21.81%	8.45%	7.52%	7.15%	0.147
LinearSVC	26.43%	7.48%	8.27%	7.24%	0.185

Table 6. Results for models trained with features constructed from the categorical attributes of defect reports from Product 2.

Classifier	Accuracy	Precision (Macro)	Recall (Macro)	F1-score (Macro)	MCC
MultinomialNB	28.72%	11.33%	13.77%	10.61%	0.267
DecisionTreeClassifier	29.3%	17.16%	18.4%	15.5%	0.273
LogisticRegression	29.47%	14.34%	16.82%	13.35%	0.275
KNeighborsClassifier	22.76%	14.66%	15.84%	13.62%	0.205
LinearSVC	**29.56%**	**14.95%**	**17.98%**	**14.33%**	**0.276**

Table 7. Results for models trained with features constructed from the textual attributes of defect reports from Product 1.

Classifier	Accuracy	Precision (Macro)	Recall (Macro)	F1-score (Macro)	MCC
MultinomialNB	47.17%	15.96%	13.35%	12.98%	0.42
DecisionTreeClassifier	39.67%	17.75%	16.86%	16.72%	0.347
LogisticRegression	55.36%	25.04%	18.56%	19.05%	0.512
KNeighborsClassifier	38.5%	17.99%	15.65%	15.57%	0.331
LinearSVC	**57.36%**	**31.61%**	**24.72%**	**26.02%**	**0.536**

Table 8. Results for models trained with features constructed from the textual attributes of defect reports from Product 2.

Classifier	Accuracy	Precision (Macro)	Recall (Macro)	F1-score (Macro)	MCC
MultinomialNB	27.12%	11.47%	8.31%	7.33%	0.245
DecisionTreeClassifier	24.67%	13.97%	13.44%	13.11%	0.226
LogisticRegression	35.12%	17.44%	13.0%	12.96%	0.328
KNeighborsClassifier	20.77%	15.75%	11.32%	11.22%	0.188
LinearSVC	**37.17%**	**23.41%**	**19.88%**	**20.07%**	**0.352**

was achieved by using **LinearSVC**. For Product 2, the maximum Accuracy of **37.17%** was achieved by using **LinearSVC**.

Tables 9 and 10 show the performance of the classification models trained with features constructed from both the categorical and textual attributes of defect reports from Product 1 and Product 2, respectively. For Product 1, the maximum Accuracy of **58.82%** was achieved by using **LinearSVC**. For Product 2, the maximum Accuracy of **48.64%** was achieved by using **LinearSVC**.

Table 9. Results for models trained with features constructed from both the textual and categorical attributes of defect reports from Product 1.

Classifier	Accuracy	Precision (Macro)	Recall (Macro)	F1-score (Macro)	MCC
MultinomialNB	48.92%	18.81%	15.83%	15.55%	0.441
DecisionTreeClassifier	39.91%	18.57%	17.75%	17.72%	0.35
LogisticRegression	56.93%	28.65%	21.12%	21.79%	0.529
KNeighborsClassifier	34.44%	16.16%	14.72%	14.32%	0.286
LinearSVC	**58.52%**	**33.93%**	**27.89%**	**28.91%**	**0.549**

Table 10. Results for models trained with features constructed from both the textual and categorical attributes of defect reports from Product 2.

Classifier	Accuracy	Precision (Macro)	Recall (Macro)	F1-score (Macro)	MCC
MultinomialNB	38.35%	22.55%	18.42%	16.8%	0.366
DecisionTreeClassifier	32.66%	23.59%	23.29%	22.61%	0.308
LogisticRegression	47.75%	34.1%	29.26%	28.68%	0.462
KNeighborsClassifier	34.25%	25.11%	25.01%	23.17%	0.324
LinearSVC	**48.64%**	**38.06%**	**35.76%**	**35.14%**	**0.472**

4.2   Predicting Multiple Components

We present the results for the recommendation system problem, where a classifier provides a list of most probable source assets as an output. For each feature set the classification model with the maximum *Recall@5* is bolded in the provided tables. The metrics *Recall@1*, *Recall@3* and *Recall@10* are also reported to show the relationship between Recall and the number of recommendations. Furthermore, the results of the feature set which provided the highest providing classifier for each product are complemented with a chart which shows the relationship between *Recall* and *Precision* for different numbers of recommendations.

Tables 11 and 12 show the performance of the classification models trained with features constructed from the categorical attributes of defect reports from

Table 11. Results for recommendation model trained with features derived from categorical attributes of defect reports from Product 1.

Classifier	Recall@1	Recall@3	Recall@5	Recall@10
MultinomialNB	26.29%	48.6%	62.54%	81.39%
DecisionTreeClassifier	25.94%	45.98%	59.37%	75.89%
LogisticRegression	**26.83%**	**48.6%**	**62.72%**	**81.66%**
KNeighborsClassifier	21.68%	37.11%	44.42%	48.56%
LinearSVC	26.36%	48.54%	62.65%	81.72%

Table 12. Results for recommendation model trained with features derived from categorical attributes of defect reports from Product 2.

Classifier	Recall@1	Recall@3	Recall@5	Recall@10
MultinomialNB	28.74%	48.12%	60.58%	79.58%
DecisionTreeClassifier	29.32%	48.58%	59.3%	75.86%
LogisticRegression	29.49%	49.91%	61.92%	80.95%
KNeighborsClassifier	23.02%	38.11%	45.03%	47.69%
LinearSVC	**29.39%**	**49.43%**	**62.35%**	**81.55%**

Product 1 and Product 2, respectively. For Product 1, the maximum Recall@5 of **62.72%** was achieved by using **LogisticRegression**. For Product 2, the maximum Accuracy of **62.35%** is achieved by using **LinearSVC**.

Tables 13 and 14 show the performance of the classification models trained with features constructed from the textual attributes of defect reports from Product 1 and Product 2, respectively. For Product 1, the maximum Recall@5 of **86.74%** is achieved by using **LinearSVC**. For Product 2, the maximum accuracy of **70.06%** is achieved by using **LinearSVC**.

Table 13. Results for recommendation model trained with features derived from textual attributes of defect reports from Product 1.

Classifier	Recall@1	Recall@3	Recall@5	Recall@10
MultinomialNB	47.16%	70.08%	79.28%	89.23%
DecisionTreeClassifier	39.86%	40.59%	41.08%	52.43%
LogisticRegression	55.35%	76.89%	84.33%	92.13%
KNeighborsClassifier	38.49%	57.08%	64.67%	68.94%
LinearSVC	**56.35%**	**78.73%**	**86.74%**	**94.03%**

Tables 15 and 16 show the performance of the classification models trained with features constructed from both the categorical and textual attributes of

Table 14. Results for recommendation model trained with features derived from textual attributes of defect reports from Product 2.

Classifier	Recall@1	Recall@3	Recall@5	Recall@10
MultinomialNB	27.12%	47.51%	58.01%	73.04%
DecisionTreeClassifier	24.83%	27.16%	28.43%	31.38%
LogisticRegression	35.11%	56.53%	66.43%	79.67%
KNeighborsClassifier	20.76%	35.31%	43.29%	45.98%
LinearSVC	**37.02%**	**60.19%**	**70.06%**	**82.9%**

defect reports from Product 1 and Product 2, respectively. For Product 1, the maximum Recall@5 of **86.59%** is achieved by using **LinearSVC**. For Product 2, the maximum accuracy of **81.9%** is achieved by using **LinearSVC**.

Table 15. Results for recommendation model trained with features derived from both the textual and categorical attributes of defect reports from Product 1.

Classifier	Recall@1	Recall@3	Recall@5	Recall@10
MultinomialNB	48.91%	70.44%	79.59%	89.06%
DecisionTreeClassifier	40.17%	40.87%	41.32%	52.31%
LogisticRegression	56.92%	77.75%	85.09%	92.63%
KNeighborsClassifier	34.43%	51.7%	59.86%	63.59%
LinearSVC	**57.91%**	**79.08%**	**86.59%**	**94.1%**

Table 16. Results for recommendation model trained with features derived from both the textual and categorical attributes of defect reports from Product 2.

Classifier	Recall@1	Recall@3	Recall@5	Recall@10
MultinomialNB	38.36%	59.19%	70.21%	84.65%
DecisionTreeClassifier	32.67%	34.95%	35.99%	38.45%
LogisticRegression	47.76%	70.54%	80.26%	91.15%
KNeighborsClassifier	34.27%	52.71%	60.04%	61.84%
LinearSVC	**48.8%**	**71.75%**	**81.9%**	**92.34%**

Figures 3 and 4 show the relationship between Recall and Precision for different numbers of recommendations of the classification models trained with features constructed from both the categorical and textual attributes of defect reports from Product 1 and Product 2, respectively. Furthermore, the figures include the values of the baseline model as a point of reference.

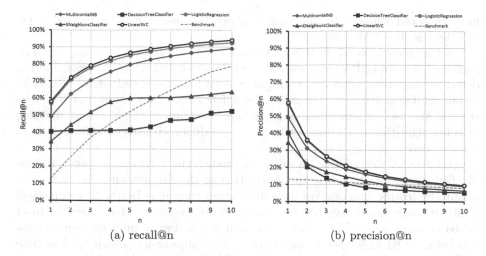

Fig. 3. Resulting (a) recall@n and (b) precision@n for recommendation model trained with features constructed from both textual and categorical attributes of defect reports from Product 1.

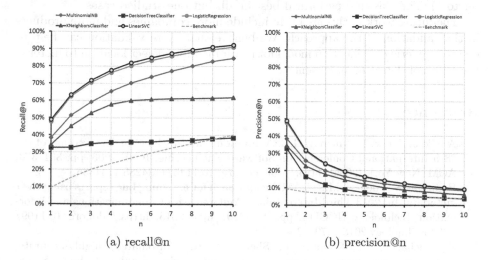

Fig. 4. Resulting (a) recall@n and (b) precision@n for recommendation model trained with features constructed from both textual and categorical attributes of defect reports from Product 2.

5   Conclusions

One of the challenges faced by software development teams, when working with defects, is the ability to find the right location of the defect. Previous studies have shown that we can predict the time when a defect can be found [20] and which team should be the most suitable one for resolving the defect [9]. The teams, however, need support to understand where the defect can be located – i.e. identify the defect locations.

In this paper, we studied how to support this process by using machine learning. We studied a large software development organization, with mature defect management processes. Our goal was to find a method to automatically recommend teams where to look for the defects once they are reported by the testers. We used a simulation study where we applied five different machine learning algorithms on a data set from two products with over 10,000 defects in the database.

Our results showed that in order to predict the location, we need to create feature vectors based on the description of the failures and the meta-data about the testing process. We have also found that it is better to recommend multiple components together with the probability rather than a single, most probable component. The accuracy of such prediction of multiple components can be up to 92.34% when recommending ten components (which are less than 25% of all components) and an accuracy of 70% can be achieved already when recommending three components. We have found that the best algorithm is the LinearSVC (Support Vector Machine with linear kernel and the cost parameter set to 1). The classifier performed best in all, but one studied cases.

The future work in this area is to include more companies and more products in the validation of the approach. We believe that more validation can help to create a generic classification model for recommending defect location to increase the speed of defect management.

References

1. Anvik, J., Hiew, L., Murphy, G.C.: Who should fix this bug? In: Proceedings of the 28th International Conference on Software Engineering, ICSE 2006, pp. 361–370. ACM, New York (2006). http://doi.acm.org/10.1145/1134285.1134336
2. Banitaan, S., Alenezi, M.: TRAM: an approach for assigning bug reports using their metadata. In: 2013 Third International Conference on Communications and Information Technology (ICCIT), pp. 215–219, June 2013. https://doi.org/10.1109/ICCITechnology.2013.6579552
3. Bhattacharya, P., Neamtiu, I., Shelton, C.R.: Automated, highly-accurate, bug assignment using machine learning and tossing graphs. J. Syst. Softw. **85**(10), 2275–2292 (2012). http://www.sciencedirect.com/science/article/pii/S0164121212001240. Automated Software Evolution
4. Bosch, J.: Speed, data, and ecosystems: the future of software engineering. IEEE Softw. **33**(1), 82–88 (2016)
5. Cavalcanti, Y.A.C., da Mota Silveira Neto, P.A., Machado, I.D.C., Vale, T.F., de Almeida, E.S., Meira, S.R.D.L.: Challenges and opportunities for software change request repositories: a systematic mapping study. J. Softw. Evol. Process **26**(7), 620–653 (2014). https://doi.org/10.1002/smr.1639. http://dx.doi.org/10.1002/smr.1639
6. Goyal, A., Sardana, N.: Machine learning or information retrieval techniques for bug triaging: which is better? e-Informatica Softw. Eng. J. **11**(1), 117–141 (2017)

7. Jalbert, N., Weimer, W.: Automated duplicate detection for bug tracking systems. In: 2008 IEEE International Conference on Dependable Systems and Networks With FTCS and DCC (DSN), pp. 52–61, June 2008. https://doi.org/10.1109/DSN.2008.4630070

8. Jonsson, L.: Increasing anomaly handling efficiency in large organizations using applied machine learning. In: 2013 35th International Conference on Software Engineering (ICSE), pp. 1361–1364, May 2013. https://doi.org/10.1109/ICSE.2013.6606717

9. Jonsson, L., Borg, M., Broman, D., Sandahl, K., Eldh, S., Runeson, P.: Automated bug assignment: ensemble-based machine learning in large scale industrial contexts. Empir. Softw. Eng. **21**(4), 1533–1578 (2016)

10. Lessmann, S., Baesens, B., Mues, C., Pietsch, S.: Benchmarking classification models for software defect prediction: a proposed framework and novel findings. IEEE Trans. Softw. Eng. **34**(4), 485–496 (2008). https://doi.org/10.1109/TSE.2008.35

11. Lin, Z., Shu, F., Yang, Y., Hu, C., Wang, Q.: An empirical study on bug assignment automation using Chinese bug data. In: 2009 3rd International Symposium on Empirical Software Engineering and Measurement, pp. 451–455, October 2009. https://doi.org/10.1109/ESEM.2009.5315994

12. Martini, A., Pareto, L., Bosch, J.: Enablers and inhibitors for speed with reuse. In: Proceedings of the 16th International Software Product Line Conference-Volume 1, pp. 116–125. ACM (2012)

13. Rana, R., Staron, M., Hansson, J., Nilsson, M., Meding, W.: A framework for adoption of machine learning in industry for software defect prediction. In: 2014 9th International Conference on Software Engineering and Applications (ICSOFT-EA), pp. 383–392, August 2014

14. Runeson, P., Alexandersson, M., Nyholm, O.: Detection of duplicate defect reports using natural language processing. In: Proceedings of the 29th International Conference on Software Engineering, ICSE 2007, pp. 499–510. IEEE Computer Society, Washington, DC (2007). https://doi.org/10.1109/ICSE.2007.32. http://dx.doi.org.proxy.lib.chalmers.se/10.1109/ICSE.2007.32

15. Sammut, C., Webb, G.I.: Encyclopedia of Machine Learning, 1st edn. Springer, Boston (2011)

16. Scikit-learn: Scikit-learn Framework. http://scikit-learn.org/stable/

17. Ståhl, D., Bosch, J.: Experienced benefits of continuous integration in industry software product development: a case study. In: The 12th IASTED International Conference on Software Engineering, Innsbruck, Austria, pp. 736–743 (2013)

18. Staron, M., Meding, W.: Predicting short-term defect inflow in large software projects: an initial evaluation. In: Proceedings of the 11th International Conference on Evaluation and Assessment in Software Engineering, EASE 2007, pp. 33–42, British Computer Society, Swinton (2007). http://dl.acm.org/citation.cfm?id=2227134.2227138

19. Staron, M., Meding, W.: Predicting weekly defect inflow in large software projects based on project planning and test status. Inf. Softw. Technol. **50**(7–8), 782–796 (2008). https://doi.org/10.1016/j.infsof.2007.10.001

20. Staron, M., Meding, W.: Predicting weekly defect inflow in large software projects based on project planning and test status. Inf. Softw. Technol. **50**(7–8), 782–796 (2008)

21. Sun, C., Lo, D., Wang, X., Jiang, J., Khoo, S.C.: A discriminative model approach for accurate duplicate bug report retrieval. In: Proceedings of the 32nd ACM/IEEE International Conference on Software Engineering - Volume 1, ICSE 2010, pp. 45–54. ACM, New York (2010). http://doi.acm.org/10.1145/1806799.1806811

22. Tian, Y., Sun, C., Lo, D.: Improved duplicate bug report identification. In: 2012 16th European Conference on Software Maintenance and Reengineering, pp. 385–390, March 2012. https://doi.org/10.1109/CSMR.2012.48
23. Xia, X., Lo, D., Wang, X., Zhou, B.: Accurate developer recommendation for bug resolution. In: 2013 20th Working Conference on Reverse Engineering (WCRE), pp. 72–81, October 2013. https://doi.org/10.1109/WCRE.2013.6671282

Source Code Analysis

Benefits and Drawbacks of Representing and Analyzing Source Code and Software Engineering Artifacts with Graph Databases

Rudolf Ramler[1](✉)[iD], Georg Buchgeher[1], Claus Klammer[1], Michael Pfeiffer[1], Christian Salomon[1], Hannes Thaller[2], and Lukas Linsbauer[2]

[1] Software Competence Center Hagenberg GmbH, Softwarepark 21,
4232 Hagenberg, Austria
{rudolf.ramler,georg.buchgeher,claus.klammer,
michael.pfeiffer,christian.salomon}@scch.at
[2] Johannes Kepler University Linz, Altenberger Street 69, 4040 Linz, Austria
{hannes.thaller,lukas.linsbauer}@jku.at
http://www.scch.at
https://www.jku.at/isse

Abstract. Source code and related artifacts of software systems encode valuable expert knowledge accumulated over many person-years of development. Analyzing software systems and extracting this knowledge requires processing the source code and reconstructing structure and dependency information. In analysis projects over the last years, we have created tools and services using graph databases for representing and analyzing source code and other software engineering artifacts as well as their dependencies. Graph databases such as Neo4j are optimized for storing, traversing, and manipulating data in the form of nodes and relationships. They are scalable, extendable, and can quickly be adapted for different application scenarios. In this paper, we share our insights and experience from five different cases where graph databases have been used as a common solution concept for analyzing source code and related artifacts. They cover a broad spectrum of use cases from industry and research, ranging from lightweight dependency analysis to analyzing the architecture of a large-scale software system with 44 million lines of code. We discuss the benefits and drawbacks of using graph databases in the reported cases. The benefits are related to representing dependencies between source code elements and other artifacts, the support for rapid prototyping of analysis solutions, and the power and flexibility of the graph query language. The drawbacks concern the generic frontends of graph databases and the lack of support for time series data. A summary of application scenarios for using graph databases concludes the paper.

Keywords: Static analysis · Dependency analysis
Knowledge extraction · Graph database · Neo4j · Experience report

ⓒ Springer Nature Switzerland AG 2019
D. Winkler et al. (Eds.): SWQD 2019, LNBIP 338, pp. 125–148, 2019.
https://doi.org/10.1007/978-3-030-05767-1_9

1   Introduction

The size and complexity of real-world software systems are continuously increasing. Today, many companies develop and maintain software systems containing hundreds or thousands of source code files encompassing up to several million lines of code. They often consist of a mix of various technologies and, additionally, a wide range of related software engineering artifacts such as tests, documentation, change requests, bug reports, and execution logs. Source code and artifacts encode valuable expert knowledge accumulated over decades of development. They represent complex structures and related information about various parts of the software system.

Nevertheless, the source code and a large part of the artifacts are stored in text files organized in conventional directory structures. Analyzing software systems requires parsing these files and reconstructing the structure and relationship information. This first step is typically the precondition for a further, more advanced analysis aiming at software understanding, interactive exploration, fault detection, visualization, and documentation. Advanced analysis applications benefit from infrastructure for processing and representing the structure of software systems in a scalable and extensible way.

In several projects developing tools and services for software analysis, we have created different implementations of such infrastructures using graph databases for representing source code, software engineering artifacts and their relationships. Graph databases [18] are NoSQL databases that support graph data models, i.e., data represented in the form of nodes connected via edges with each other. Graph databases are particularly useful if relationships between nodes are a central characteristic of the stored data. They are optimized for storing, querying, and manipulating vast amounts of highly connected data by native support for relationships and enhanced traversal capabilities. Hence, they are frequently used in a wide range of applications such as recommendation engines, social networks, collaboration platforms, and medical research systems.

The objective of this paper is to collect and share our experiences with graph databases in representing and analyzing source code and software engineering artifacts. We describe five different cases related to different application scenarios and project contexts. Across all cases, the use of graph databases has emerged as a common element in the implemented solutions – yet with variations in how the data is modeled, stored and accessed. By comparing and discussing the different approaches, data models, and underlying design decisions, we provide insights into the advantages and disadvantages of graph databases for building analysis tools and services.

The remainder of the paper is structured as follows. Section 2 provides an introduction to graph databases and outlines related work. The research design of our experience report is described in Sect. 3. Details about the five presented cases are described in Sect. 4. The discussion of identified advantages and disadvantages follows in Sect. 5. Finally, Sect. 6 concludes the paper by summarizing the key findings and suggestions for future work.

2   Background and Related Work

A graph is composed of nodes and relationships. A node represents an entity (e.g., `class`, `method` or `variable`) and a relationship represents how two nodes are associated (e.g., a class `contains` a method, a method `calls` a method or `reads` a variable). Nodes and relationships can have properties that are usually specified in form of key-value-pairs (e.g., `name='foo'`). This general-purpose concept enables creating arbitrary connected structures that closely match the modeled characteristics of the problem domain [4].

A graph database is an online database management system with `create`, `read`, `update` and `delete` operations optimized for graph data models [18]. Graph databases are specifically designed to support fast and scalable management, storage, and traversal of nodes and relationships. This support allows to specify all relationships representing connections between entities at the time the data is created, and storing them persistently in the database. When the database is queried, these relations can be quickly traversed without the need to compute them dynamically via foreign keys and costly join operations.

The widespread adoption of NoSQL databases for many problem domains also led to the development of several databases specialized on graph data. Examples include AllegroGraph (Franz Inc.), InfiniteGraph (Objectivity Inc.), Neo4j (Neo4j Technology Inc.), and OrientDB (Callidus Software Inc.). A review and comparison of contemporary graph databases can be found in [3].

The cases we describe in this paper use the graph database *Neo4j*[1]. It is one of the most popular graph databases, also offered open source. Neo4j is based on a native graph storage and processing engine. It comes with the declarative graph query language *Cypher* that supports the definition, manipulation, and querying of graphs. Cypher queries can be issued using programming language specific drivers or the Web-based user interface *Neo4j browser*. In addition, Neo4j supports a programming language independent REST API and a low-level Java driver that can directly access database search facilities.

Many approaches and tools exist for analyzing software systems [13] and for performing queries on source code [1]. Most of these approaches and tools rely on database technologies to store structure and dependency information. Although the use of relational databases is still prevalent, NoSQL databases are receiving more and more attention. Zhang et al. [24] implemented a framework for querying heterogeneous code repositories using the document-oriented database MongoDB.

Graph databases have been applied in a few instances, by Yamaguchi et al. [22] for analyzing code to discover vulnerabilities, by Urma and Mycroft [21] for querying source code, by Goonetilleke et al. [8] to implement the tool Frappe for code comprehension, and in the open source tool jQAssistant[2] for ensuring code quality of Java programs. These applications are related to the cases described

---

[1]   https://neo4j.com.
[2]   https://jqassistant.org.

in our study. However, an analysis of large-scale software systems similar to what we present in our case study has only been described for Frappe [9].

3 Research Design

This paper reports our insights and experiences gained from using graph databases in the form of a collection of individual cases. Each case provides a first-hand account by the authors, who have been personally involved in the reported cases and the development of the associated tools and services.

Research goals and questions: Besides describing *how graph databases are used*, the paper explores *what are the advantages* and *what are the disadvantage* of using graph databases for representing and analyzing source code and related artifacts.

We conducted the following steps to provide answers to these questions.

1. **Case selection:** The key criteria for selecting a case to be included in our report were the use of a graph database, its application for supporting software analysis tasks, and the development of related tools or services.
2. **Case description:** We used a template with a uniform structure related to a set of open questions to describe the cases. The descriptions were prepared by the authors involved in the cases.
3. **Review of descriptions:** The case descriptions were reviewed by co-authors not involved in the case to assure that the descriptions are complete and consistent. Variations and extensions to the structure of the descriptions were introduced to capture individual aspects of the reported cases.
4. **Compile overview:** A table showing the essential characteristics of all reported cases was prepared for comparing the cases and for identifying their commonalities and individualities.
5. **Exploration of individual cases:** The cases were discussed and explored further w.r.t. design decisions, encountered challenges, open issues, and feedback from users. The findings were the basis for deriving a list of advantages, disadvantages, and lessons learned for each case.
6. **Synthesis of findings:** The findings from the individual cases were aggregated to high-level advantages and disadvantages as well as general lessons learned for presentation in the paper.

Several measures were taken to mitigate threats to validity. We decided to select multiple cases with different characteristics to support generalization. The information about the cases was provided by authors who were personally involved. To reduce the resulting bias, we used a shared template for preparing case descriptions, which were then reviewed and discussed with authors not directly involved in the cases.

Nevertheless, analyzing cases does not always allow to accurately identify the boundary between the observed phenomenon and the context [19]. The advantages, disadvantages and lessons learned we identified in our work may therefore still depend on influence factors rooted in the specific project or application context. To counter this threat, we decided to put the primary focus of this paper on the presentation of the individual cases to support the reader in transferring the insights and experiences to his/her own context.

4   Description of Cases

The five presented cases (*Case 1–5*) cover a variety of different applications scenarios related to the analysis of source code and related artifacts. Each of them is based on a unique goal and motivation, derived from its application in industry projects[3] or research. The common theme shared by all cases is the implementation of tool support and services for which graph databases have been applied. Table 1 provides an overview of the key characteristics of the five cases, summarizing the spectrum of different applications realized with graph databases.

In the subsections below, the descriptions of the cases are based on the following structure.

- **Project context:** In what application scenarios is the graph database used?
- **Data model:** What data model is used to represent the structure and relationships of the analyzed source code or software engineering artifacts?
- **Data sources:** How is the data created and imported into the database?
- **Access and usage:** How is the data in the database accessed and used?
- **Status and ongoing work:** What is the current state of the work and what are the next steps?

4.1   Case 1: AutoDoc for Lightweight Dependency Analysis

AutoDoc is a lightweight and flexible dependency analysis tool based on static code analysis for various programming languages.

Project Context: The tool has been developed in a project with industry partners from the domain of embedded systems. These systems have to fulfill high quality demands. The project supported the industry partners in improving software quality by providing unit testing and source code analysis technology. AutoDoc statically analyzes the source code of the software system and generates information about components and their interrelations. Furthermore, a set of code-related metrics is calculated including Halstead, McCabe complexity, and the Microsoft maintainability index. The results are used by developers in various ways, for example, to gain an overview of interdependencies between the units of a software system, to determine areas for refactoring and testability improvements, or to estimate the impact of architectural changes. By using a language agnostic parsing frontend, the tool is applicable for systems implemented in various different programming languages; currently, it is used to analyze systems implemented in C.

---

[3] If not already revealed in previous publications, details about involved industry partners have been omitted due to confidentiality obligations.

Table 1. Overview of the Reported Cases.

	AutoDoc	SCoRe	eKNOWS CMS	Sherlock	Gradient
Goal and motivation	Lightweight, flexible, customizable code analysis	Analyzing industrial PLC software	Service for reusable static code analysis	Dependency analysis for regression test selection	Probabilistic software modeling
Application context	Industry projects	Industry projects	Industry projects	Industry projects	Research prototype
Represented source code or artifacts	Call, read, and write dependencies in various languages (currently C)	PLC programs written in IEC 61131-3 languages	Java systems (from high-level config to source code statements)	Source code structure (C++, C#), code changes, system tests, test coverage	Static code structure and models of behavior (Java VM languages)
Users	Developers	Developers, software architects	Developers of software engineering tools and services	Software testers, quality and release managers	Researchers, developers
Usage scenarios	Analysis of dependencies enriched with metrics	Design and architecture review, support for refactoring	Analysis of large-scale systems, evolution analysis	Selecting regression tests for source code changes	Program comprehension and behavioral analysis
Data access and user interfaces	Neo4j Web interface	Neo4j Web interface	Different (3rd party) tools, REST API	Custom client, export to test tool	Custom Web interface
Data sources	Source code files	Source code files	Version control systems (VCS)	VCS, task management, coverage analysis, test management	Source code, execution traces from run-time
Schema size (distinct elements)	2 node types, 6 relationship types, 9 metric values	24 node types, 15 relationship types	83 node types, 88 relationship types	9 node types, 15 relationship types	11 node types, 20 relationship types
Size of analyzed system	72,000 LOC C code	742,000 LOC IEC61131-3	44 million LOC Java	2.5 million LOC C++ and C#	n.a.
Data import/update strategy	Import, existing data replaced	Bulk import, existing data replaced	Cyclic builds, data partially updated	Nightly and manual updates, data partially replaced	Triggered builds with incremental updates

Data Model: AutoDoc stores dependency analysis results as graph into the Neo4j database. The data model is depicted in Fig. 1. It models dependencies due to function calls and field access. The nodes are of type `function` or `field`. Relations of type `calls` exist between functions; `reads`, `writes`, `read_writes`, or `indirect_writes` relations between functions and fields. The more abstract indirect_writes relations show that a member of a field is written by a function. Metrics values, e.g., complexity measures, are stored as attributes for function nodes.

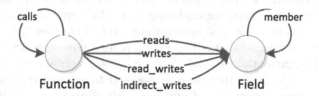

Fig. 1. Data model of AutoDoc.

Data Sources: The foundation of the tool is the general-purpose code analysis platform part of SCCH's eKNOWS tool family [7], which is used in different projects in the field of static code analysis, domain knowledge extraction, and re-documentation. The platform provides parser frontends for numerous programming languages to transform the code into the Generic Abstract Syntax Tree Model (GASTM). The generic representation allows to make downstream transformations and additional analyses available for any of the supported programming languages. AutoDoc utilizes the C code parser frontend of eKNOWS to transform the code into its GASTM representation (Fig. 2). Call graph and dependencies are calculated from this model. The resulting graph is stored in the Neo4j graph database. Analysis runs are triggered either manually on demand or periodically by integrating the tool into the build process.

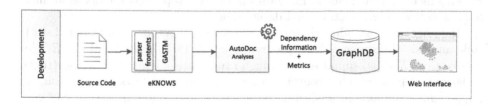

Fig. 2. System overview AutoDoc.

Access and Usage: The data stored in the graph database is accessed via the standard Neo4j Web interface, which supports users in exploring the analysis results by writing queries or executing previously saved queries. We provide predefined queries to answer common questions with respect to system components, dependencies, and accessed variables, for example, *"How often are global*

*variables accessed?", "What global variables are written by different functions?",
"What functions access many different global variables?", "What are the most
complex functions?", or "Which functions have a high maintainability index?".*
The typical target audience of AutoDoc are developers performing a detailed
analysis of the system under development. We found that these users are comfortable with formulating ad-hoc queries using the easy to understand Cypher
query language.

Status and Ongoing Work: AutoDoc is currently used by our industry partners in two main ways, first, for exploring and refactoring of legacy code and,
second, for continuous code quality assurance. While the Neo4j browser seems
sufficient for the first use case, the generation of an analysis report is considered
for the later. The currently analyzed software systems contain up to 72,000 lines
of embedded C code. Nevertheless, it is planned to expand the application of
AutoDoc to analyzing a system of systems with more than a million lines of
code.

4.2   Case 2: SCoRe for PLC Programs

SCoRe is a static analysis tool developed explicitly for analyzing PLC programs
written in IEC 61131-3 programming languages for industrial automation and
production systems.

Project Context: The programming languages defined by the IEC 61131-3
standard [11] are used in industry to implement the control software of real-time
systems. The software runs on dedicated hardware, i.e., programmable logic
controllers (PLCs). Due to the focus on a relatively small niche, these software
systems have received little attention in the past. Only a few software engineering
tools are available, mainly proprietary programming environments tied to PLCs
of specific vendors. However, the size and complexity of today's industrial control
systems increased the demand for additional tools supporting quality assurance,
testing, software architecture, and design tasks.

Together with our industry partners, we developed a tool for automated static
code analysis of large-scale PLC programs (c.f. [2,15,16]). The tool *SCoRe* (for
Source Code Review) supports detecting a range of problematic code constructs,
violations of programming conventions, and potential defects. In addition, we
implemented support for analyzing the software design and architecture of control systems by exporting the structure and dependency information extracted in
static code analysis available to the graph database Neo4j. This solution allows
exploring and examining the various program elements and their dependencies
via custom queries and by browsing the graph visualization in the Neo4j Web
interface. Figure 3 provides an overview of the tool chain. It distinguishes the
tool's application in *implementation* for automated static code analysis based
on a set of predefined rules from *design and architecture analysis*, which requires
support for interactively exploring and reviewing the software system.

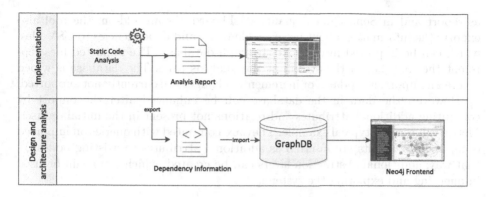

Fig. 3. Overview and usage of SCoRe.

Data Model: The Neo4j database contains 24 distinct node types that represent the various building blocks commonly used in PLC programs [11]. They are structured into **functional units** that contain **program units** (e.g., function blocks or functions) and define **system variables**. Program units can **call** other program units, **read** and **write** system variables, and to **send events** or **listen for events**. Instances of program units are assigned to process **tasks** for execution in cyclic intervals. Figure 4 provides an overview of the most important building blocks (nodes) and their dependencies (relations). Nodes can contain additional attributes such as the path to the source code files or optional metric values (e.g., number of imports, or fan-in and fan-out).

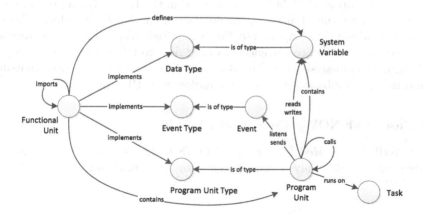

Fig. 4. Data model of SCoRe.

Data Sources: The SCoRe tool parses the PLC program, constructs the abstract syntax tree, the control flow graph, and the data flow graph. The predefined rules are used to detect issues in the source code, which are then listed as report and in SonarQube's quality dashboard. As an add-on, the tool also exports the information about program elements and dependencies to CSV files, which can be imported into the Neo4j graph database. The imported files represent the snapshot of the system at the analysis time. The database is wiped before an import, as updates or incremental changes are currently not supported.

However, the data in the database can be enhanced after the import by computing additional attributes and relations not present in the initial dataset. Metric values are a typical example. They are computed with queries on imported data, and the results are inserted as additional attributes to existing nodes. In that way, additional abstraction layers can be created, which can again be used in querying and exploring the system.

Access and Usage: The generic Neo4j Web frontend is used to for submitting custom Cypher queries and interactive exploration of result graphs. It can be easily accessed by all members of the development team as only a Web browser is required. Together with our industry partners we identified the following application scenarios for SCoRe: Evaluating the compliance of the implementation with design decisions and guidelines (e.g., use of global variables), computing metrics (e.g., coupling and cohesion), support for refactoring (e.g., identifying large program units), and analyzing the potential impact of changes (e.g., dependencies on changed elements).

Status and Ongoing Work: The tool SCoRe is currently applied by two industry partners developing industrial automation systems. It has been used to analyze systems up to 742 KLOC implemented in the IEC 61131-3 programming languages, which resulted in about 450,000 nodes and 2,500,000 relationships in the graph database. The import into Neo4j required 21.4 seconds on a standard desktop computer. We are currently working on extending the tool to support the simultaneous analysis of IEC 61131-3 and C/C++ as our industry partners are also using a combination of both technologies in PLC programs.

4.3   Case 3: eKNOWS Code Model Service

The *eKNOWS Code Model Service* (eKNOWS CMS) is a service that provides reusable static code analysis functionality for Java programs via a dedicated REST API.

Project Context: eKNOWS CMS has been developed as the foundation of a microservice-based system for extracting architectural information from large-scale service-oriented software systems via static code analysis [6]. The system has been developed in close cooperation with Raiffeisen Software GmbH (RSG), a provider of IT solutions for the finance domain in Austria.

System Overview: Figure 5 depicts an overview of the eKNOWS CMS. As shown in the figure, eKNOWS CMS is implemented as a microservice that provides static code analysis functionality to a set of other microservices and tools. These analyses are provided via a dedicated Representational State Transfer (REST) API. Static code analysis in the eKNOWS CMS differs from many other code analysis approaches where analysis is performed via abstract syntax tree (AST) visitors for deriving information from the system implementation. Instead, we have implemented static code analysis by means of Cypher queries. We provide the following kinds of analyses:

- Search for type and interface declarations of a specified module.
- Search for type, field, and method declarations with specified metadata.
- Search for extended types and implemented interfaces of a specified type declaration, search for all type declarations derived from a specified type, and search for all type declarations implementing a specified interface.
- Search for import relationships of a specified module, and search for modules importing a specified module.
- Search for method declarations of types and interfaces.
- Calculation of call graphs and caller graphs for specified method declarations
- Search for XML documents and elements and attributes of XML documents
- Search for MANIFEST files and their attributes
- Calculation of type dependency relationships.

On top of the eKNOWS CMS we have developed a set of services that use the provided code analysis functionality. These services then provide information to different tools used at RSG. A detailed description of the developed services and used tools can be found in [6].

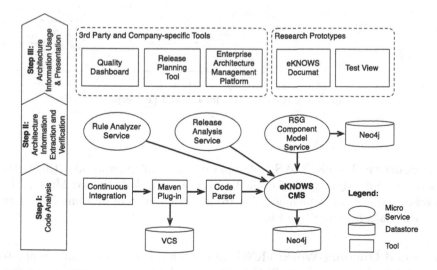

Fig. 5. eKNOWS code model service - System overview

Data Model: Figure 6 depicts an excerpt of the data model of the eKNOWS CMS. The data model consists of 83 different node and 88 relationship types that are used for storing complete **implementation artifacts** (i.e., source code, XML, and Manifest files) in Neo4j by converting these artifacts into graph structures. All implementation artifacts are assigned to a dedicated **module**, which is the unit of versioning and deployment. Modules define dependencies to other modules via **import relationships**. The eKNOWS CMS can store multiple **versions** of the system implementation in Neo4j, i.e., we store all released versions of a module along with the version of the current development iteration that is overwritten whenever a cyclic build process is triggered. Modules can be aggregated to **applications** to describe modular systems. Finally, we also store the results of resource-intensive analyses, i.e., call graphs and dependencies between types in Neo4j to avoid redundant analyses.

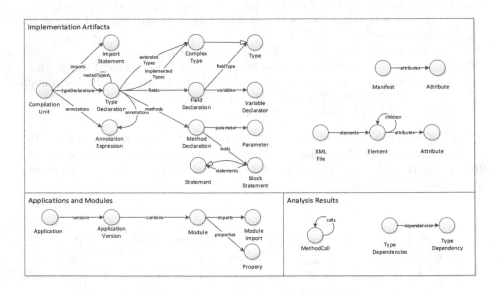

Fig. 6. eKNOWS CMS data model (Excerpt).

Data Sources: The eKNOWS CMS operates on implementation artifacts that are written to Neo4j as part of cyclic build processes. A dedicated Maven Plug-in fetches the system implementation from version control systems (VCS) and stores this data in Neo4j (see Fig. 5).

Status and Ongoing Work: eKNOWS CMS has been successfully evaluated in an industrial case study at RSG in which we have analyzed the entire code-base of RSG's latest online banking solution (see [6]). We have analyzed over 44 million lines of code, which were stored as 138,595,573 nodes and 138,141,947 relationships in Neo4j. The correlation between the number of nodes and relationships results from the fact that we store implementation structures 1:1 in the database without relationships between implementation artifacts. Such relationships are either calculated on demand (e.g., inheritance and implemented interfaces relationships), or they are stored as dedicated data structures (e.g., call graphs and type dependencies) where references are defined via node IDs.

Currently, we are working on supporting additional use cases of stakeholders at RSG by providing corresponding architecture information using the analysis functionality of eKNOWS CMS. We will further extend the eKNOWS CMS with additional kinds of analyses to improve our support for automated generation of viewpoint-based software architecture documentation.

4.4 Case 4: Sherlock for Regression Test Case Selection

Sherlock is a tool that supports regression test case selection in manual system testing based on test coverage and code changes.

Project Context: Regression testing [23] is performed after making changes to an existing software system to ensure that these changes do not have unexpected adverse side effects on the behavior of existing, unchanged parts of the software system. The straightforward approach to regression testing is to re-execute all existing test cases to make sure they still pass. However, many software projects have a large number of test cases, and it is often impossible to re-execute all of them every time a change has been made. Regression test case selection aims at selecting a reasonably small subset of the existing test cases, which still has a high chance of detecting any issues introduced by changes.

We developed the tool *Sherlock* for selecting regression test cases based on a list of locations in the source code where changes have been made and the information which test cases cover these source code locations [5]. Sherlock specifically supports interactively selecting test cases for manual regression testing in the context of a large-scale software product by OMICRON electronics GmbH. This software product encompasses more than 30 modules (about 2.5 MLOC in total, mostly implemented in C++) that interact with each other and share a common framework as well as various base libraries and hardware drivers. The system has grown to its current size over a time span of more than two decades. Engineers in different roles (i.e., developers, architects) have contributed over time, creating a large and sophisticated software system with complex dependencies between application modules, framework components, custom interfaces, and various third-party libraries. Thus, today, one of the foremost challenges of effective and efficient regression testing lies in acquiring and managing the knowledge about the huge amount of dependencies in the software system.

Data Sources: As regression testing is a time-consuming activity [12], Sherlock helps to reduce required efforts and costs by concentrating on those tests, which exercise the parts of the system that are affected by changes. For identifying and selecting the relevant test cases, Sherlock incorporates information from three data sources (as shown in Fig. 7):

1. Information about source code and changes (e.g., check-ins) is extracted from the *version control system* of Microsoft's Team Foundation Server (TFS).
2. The list of available test cases and their properties are retrieved from the *test management system* SilkCentral Test Manager.
3. The relationship between test cases and code changes is determined from coverage analysis results produced by the *profiler* SmartBear AQtime Pro.

Custom implemented adapters based on Neo4jClient binding for .NET are used to extract, transform and load (via a bulk Cypher import) this information into a *Neo4j graph database* that acts as Sherlock's central data store.

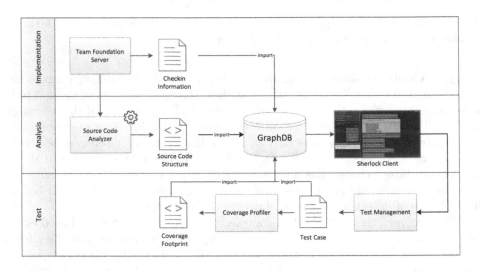

Fig. 7. Sherlock system overview.

Data Model: Sherlock stores the data in a tool-agnostic graph format (Fig. 8). Central information in the Sherlock data model are nodes holding information about all `methods` in the system under test, including details such as name or line numbers stored as attributes. Methods are grouped by `files` and are part of one or more `change-sets` (check-ins performed by a `developer`). A change-set in TFS may be connected to a `work item` that contains either a task, bug, or feature description, and which is assigned to a `software release`. A method is furthermore connected to a `regression test case` if it is part of the test's coverage footprint, i.e., if the method is called during the execution of this test case.

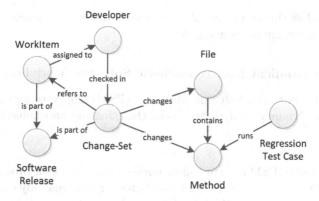

Fig. 8. Sherlock data model.

Access and Usage: Sherlock supports the testers in selecting the minimal set of regression tests to target the changes made by the developers. Therefore the testers access the aggregated information stored in the graph database using a rich client application. For compiling a regression test suite, the client application implements several Cypher queries so that testers can identify test cases related to an individual change (e.g., a bug fix), for all changes within a specified time range (e.g., all fixes and enhancements combined in a maintenance release), or all changes made on a branch before it is merged back into the trunk (e.g., all changes made while implementing a new feature). The resulting set of test cases is the basis for subsequent regression test runs scheduled from within the test management system. Sherlock provides an export interface to update the test plans in the test management system accordingly. In addition, the tool also supports the analysis of the available test cases in general. For example, it indicates coverage gaps when changed source code is not covered by the set of selected test cases or any test at all.

Status and Ongoing Work: Initially, the project started with test case selection based on static code analysis results [5], but experiments showed that in this case, static analysis approaches are not able to reveal enough dependencies relevant for test case selection, e.g., because of multi-language interoperability or reflection mechanisms. For this reason, code coverage information was collected to expose dynamic dependencies as well. Today, check-in information and source code structure are kept up-to-date by a Windows service that runs on a daily basis. This service uses custom adapters to import 21,000 check-ins and more than 200,000 methods that are grouped in 20,000 files. Coverage foot-prints for currently 400 tests are imported and updated manually after a test case was successfully profiled. Sherlock is a valuable aid for providing guidance in selecting appropriate regression test cases for testers who lack detailed knowledge of the structure and dependencies of the system under test. In an evaluation, we found that a junior tester using Sherlock was able to produce test suites with less or equal effort and at the same level of accuracy as highly experienced testers who accomplished the same tasks manually [17].

4.5   Case 5: Gradient for Probabilistic Software Modeling

Gradient is a Probabilistic Software Modeling (PSM) [20] system prototype that uses static and dynamic analysis to model the structure and behavior of a program.

Project Context: PSM systems allow engineers to inspect a program's structure (Types, Properties, Executables) *and* behavior (runtime objects) using statistical models. These statistical models can be used in applications such as visualization of runtime behavior (e.g., possible values of property `age` form a `Person` class), finding the most likely value combination of the parameters of an executable or test-case generation. The program structure is extracted via static code analysis while the behavior observations are extracted via dynamic code analysis. The static and dynamic information is then used to build a network of probabilistic models with similar behavior as the original program. The objective of Gradient is to empower software engineers with the possibility of behavioral analysis of programs without switching the level of abstraction (Types, Properties, Executables) or to content themselves with a single execution trace (e.g., debugging).

System Overview: Gradient leverages static and dynamic code analysis and builds a network of models that mirror the system under inspection. Naturally, it needs multiple stages, components, and technologies to work.

Figure 9 shows an overview of the Gradient system that is split into two parts, the client- and server-side, operating on three levels: Development, Runtime, and Modeling. First, ① the program structure is extracted from the *Source Code* and stored directly into the *Graph Database* (Neo4j) ②. Then the source code is compiled and patched with monitoring aspects that execute the monitoring logic. The *Patched Byte code* ④, containing additional monitoring logic, directly stores *Runtime Events* into the *Document Database* (MongoDB). This entire process is handled by the Gradient client which in addition reports (not shown in Fig. 9) the analysis progress to the Gradient server. This client is provided to users in the form of Gradle [10] (build tool) plugin that handles the entire tool-chain in a non-intrusive and transparent fashion. The Gradient Server than retrieves the structural and behavioral data from the databases and combines them into statistical models ⑥. The *Structure* of the program is retrieved from Neo4j along with the respective *Runtime Events* from MongoDB. The resulting models are stored back in the databases for later use where Neo4j stores the *Model Metadata* and MongoDB the raw model data. At last, the *Gradient Frontend*, hosted on the Gradient Server as a web application, can be used to access the statistical models to inspect the behavior of the analyzed program.

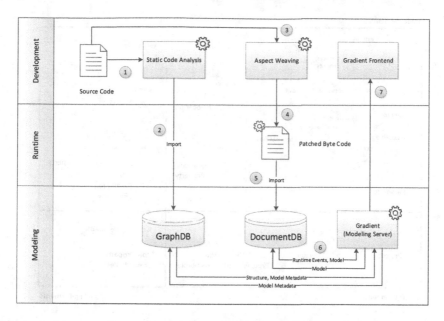

Fig. 9. Source code is statically analyzed and stored in the graph database. Furthermore, it is compiled, and the resulting byte code is patched with monitoring code that reports runtime events to the document database. Both, structure and runtime events are combined into a statistical model that is written back to the database for later analysis.

Data Model: Gradient uses a generic high-level data model that can be split into roughly three categories 1. *Code Elements*, 2. *Project Elements* and, 3. *Model Elements*, where the digest of it is shown in Fig. 10. Code Elements are related to the source code data model. Project Elements give code elements a project context and enable model versioning. Model Elements capture additional concepts related to the statistical models.

The *Code Elements* section in Fig. 10 shows that the Gradient data model has a higher level of abstraction than the traditional Abstract Syntax Tree (AST) as it only considers *Types, Properties, and Executables*. In compensation, the data model introduces *Invocation* and *Access* nodes as explicit relationship concepts that are only implicitly captured on a statement level in an AST. Another addition is the *ElementType* that allows direct access to typing information of typed elements, which cannot be straightforwardly retrieved from an AST.

Project Elements section contains *Project* nodes and *Version* nodes used to manage different projects registered on the same Gradient server. Type, Property, Executable are also *Versionables* containing a version hash that, along with their qualified name, uniquely identifies them within a project and its versions.

This also enables the database to reuse *Versionables*, along their associated statistical models, with the same qualified names and version hash across different versions. *Modeling Elements* attach model specific information to code

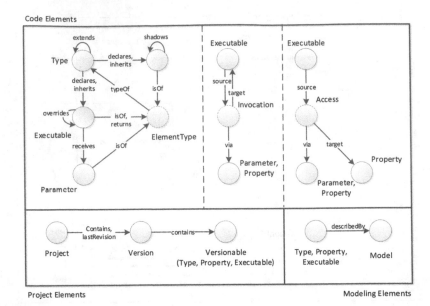

Fig. 10. The graph data model is split into 3 categories: Code Elements, Project Elements, Model Elements. Code Elements model source code concepts, Project Elements model project and versioning concepts, and Modeling Elements model concepts related to the statistical models built by Gradient.

elements that are modeled. For example, *Model* contains the id of the statistical model stored in the MongoDB.

Data Sources: Gradient has two sources of data, 1. Static code analysis on the source code, 2. Dynamic code analysis executed by the patched byte code. The static analysis parses the source code via Spoon [14] and transforms it into the Gradient model. This graph is then written into Neo4j providing the structure. The dynamic analysis is executed by the patched byte code that contains instructions to write monitoring events into the MongoDB. Neo4j can also be thought of an index database where each interaction starts by retrieving specific nodes that point to raw data in MongoDB. This raw data can be millions of runtime events, each being a JSON document or binary data of the statistical models.

Access and Usage: Gradient allows engineers to interact with their source code by inspecting the behavior of types, properties or executables. Neo4j in this setting is used as a persistent data structure of the source code that reflects the parts that are exposed to the user, and as index database for binary data stored in MongoDB. Engineers that use Gradient interact mainly via a graph in list or visual form with the statistical models, or via pre-configured queries and tasks that fully abstract the structure.

Status and Ongoing Work: Gradient is an ongoing research prototype for Java to demonstrate the feasibility of Probabilistic Software Modeling. It currently implements the static and dynamic analysis as most parts of the statistical modeling and simple views to view structure, models, and the raw data. High priority features for the future are tools for test-case generation, anomaly detection, and a frontend that allows simple interaction with the models for software developers unfamiliar with statistical modeling. Also, interactions between statistical models of different versions of the source systems are part of the future work.

5 Discussion

This section summarizes the insights and lessons learned from the five reported cases via a discussion of advantages and disadvantages of using graph databases. In each case, slightly different aspects of often the same advantage or disadvantage were observed. We therefore aggregated the individual findings collected from the different cases into high-level statements. For each of these statements, examples describing the experienced benefits and drawbacks are given, including references to the cases where they have been found.

5.1 Advantages

Graph databases (e.g., Neo4j in our case) are a suitable choice for *storing and querying the data extracted from source code and related artifacts.*

+ Graphs are a natural way to represent the manifold dependencies that are omnipresent in software systems. Working with dependencies has been an essential motivation and was often the central aspect of the tools we developed (*Case 1–5*).
+ Graph databases can handle data from large-scale software systems up to several millions of lines of code as demonstrated by *Case 3*. The limit of Graph databases rather lies in the type of data that has to be processed. For log-like execution data as in *Case 5* a document-centered database (e.g., MongoDB) is preferable; in this case, both databases were used in combination.

Graph databases provide excellent *support for rapid prototyping and exploring different options* for working with artifacts from software engineering. This advantage derives from NoSQL databases being schema-less and highly extensible.

+ Building tools on top of graph databases allow to start using them early, while still under development, and to advance the tools and the underlying data model whenever new requirements or usage scenarios are encountered (*Case 1–5*).
+ In *Case 4* the Neoclipse plugin for Eclipse has been used in a first prototype to demonstrate the integrating of the tool Sherlock into the development environment.

+ In all five cases presented above the implemented tools emerged out of research projects, where the initial versions of the tools were repeatedly revised and successively extended, e.g., to match the diverse needs of our industry partners (*Case 1–4*).

Graph query languages (e.g., Cypher in our case) provide a powerful and simple way to understand, retrieve, and manipulate graphs representing source code or related artifacts.

+ Structured processing of code and other artifacts was found to be easier when using the expressiveness of graph queries than with conventional, programmatic approaches (*Case 2* and *3*). For instance, searching the AST for all method call expressions of a particular method declaration can be achieved by a simple query instead of implementing an AST visitor that requires visiting all method call expressions of a compilation unit and determining for each expression if it belongs to the specified method declaration by checking all parent elements until a method declaration expression is found.
+ In *Case 1* and *Case 2*, the users of our tools were developers. For them, it was straightforward to write queries after a short introduction to the Cypher query language. Dozens of queries have been created so far, supporting a wide range of common analysis tasks. The queries are stored as scripts that can be easily shared and adapted to new analysis tasks.
+ The standard Neo4j Web frontend was used for querying the graph structure and to retrieve the required information about the analyzed software system. Therefore it was not necessary to develop a dedicated client or user interface in *Case 1* and *Case 2*.

5.2 Disadvantages

The *generic frontends* available for graph databases (e.g., Web-based Neo4j browser) are often not adequate for supporting end users in performing the specific tasks involved in the studied cases. Custom user interfaces had to be implemented for several of our tools.

− The standard Web interface of Neo4j provides a convenient way to submit queries to the database and to review the results using a visualization of the graph. Nevertheless, the dynamic visualization makes it difficult to maintain the overview when working with large result sets containing dependency data (*Case 1* and *Case 2*). Alternative clients (e.g., yFiles Neo4j Explorer) offer improved layouts and comfortable filtering, but the inherent weaknesses of a generic solution remain.
− Support for specific graphical representations cannot always be provided. In *Case 2*, for example, company partners suggested to display all program elements implemented in the same unit grouped using visual containers (e.g., boxes) representing these units. In contrast, a generic visualization will show the "implemented in" relationship as lines connecting each of the program elements with nodes representing the units.

- The generic user interface does not provide any guidance for users to perform tasks step by step, e.g., in selecting test cases based on a previous selection of a set of code changes (*Case 4*).
- Available frontends are usually restricted to explore data of only one graph database. It is not possible to connect data from two or more databases running in parallel or from an external data source, e.g., when combining the static structure of a software system with code changes (*Case 4*) or its dynamic behavior (*Case 5*).

Graph databases show a *lack of support for time series data*. This deficiency can be attributed to their specialization on graph data and the philosophy followed by many NoSQL databases, which is "do one thing and do it well". Neo4j, as we used it in our cases, does not offer any features specific for storing or querying time series data.

- In modeling software engineering artifacts, however, time-related dependencies play a major role due to the evolutionary and incremental approach in which software is developed. Thus, we had to develop graph models that can represent a specific combination of code, artifacts, and dependencies at a particular point in time, e.g., by relating them to dedicated nodes representing software releases or versions (*Case 3–5*).
- In *Case 4*, some of the nodes (e.g., work items) also contain timestamps as attributes, which were required to formulate queries with an additional `where` clause to retrieve all elements in a specific time span.
- In *Case 5*, log-like time series data from execution is stored in a separate database. The characteristic property of such data is the sequential ordering of the entries, which are recorded over time.
- Time points are also relevant in *Case 1* and *Case 2*. However, in these cases, the pragmatic solution was to store only a snapshot of the software system at a particular point in time in the graph database. For analyzing another snapshot, e.g., a new build or version, the entire data set has to be replaced. Managing the dependencies to builds, releases, versions, etc. is left to the users applying the tools.

6   Summary and Conclusions

In this paper, we described our experiences and lessons learned from building software analysis tools and services based on graph databases. We presented five different cases related to different application scenarios and project contexts. Each of the five cases (*Case 1–5*) is an example showing that graph databases can be effectively used for representing and analyzing source code and software engineering artifacts. The diversity as well as the size and complexity of the reported cases underpin this finding.

A *broad range of program elements* is stored in the form nodes and relationships in the graph databases. They range from dependencies such as function calls and read/write access to variables (*Case 1*) to the entire AST of large-scale software systems (*Case 3*). Software written in *various programming languages* has been represented as graphs, e.g., C, C++, C#, Java, and IEC 61131-3 languages (*Case 1–5*). The resulting *size and complexity of the graph structures* range from only two distinct node types and 6 distinct relationship types (*Case 1*) to 83 node types and 88 different relationship types (*Case 3*).

The graph databases showed a high level of *scalability* when used for analyzing up to 44 million lines of code at the level of individual syntax elements. The resulting graph contained more than 138 million nodes and about the same amount of relationships, which were stored in the database (*Case 3*).

The graph models were used for capturing the data extracted from various *different artifacts*: Source code files (*Case 1–5*); system configurations in form of XML files (*Case 3*); work items, check-ins, software tests, and coverage information (*Case 4*); project and version information (*Case 3–5*).

The databases are populated in a single initial import replacing existing data (*Case 1–2*) or they are updated in increments partially extending the data in the database (*Case 3–5*). The various approaches for accessing the data include Neo4j's standard Web interface (*Case 1–2*), custom built client applications (*Case 3–5*), a REST API (*Case 3*), and an export interface (*Case 4*).

The insights and lessons learned we collected from using graph databases have been compiled into a list of advantages and disadvantages to support decisions in related and future applications.

The key *advantages*, relevant for choosing graph databases as storage option in software analysis, are related to the *versatility of the graph data model*. It was found suitable to represent all kind of structures and relations usually encountered in software systems. It can be used to represent dependencies between individual program elements as well as for links across technology boundaries. In addition, the flexibility and scalability of graph databases provide an ideal basis for *prototyping and evolving analysis solutions*. Finally, *specialized graph query languages* are a powerful yet easy to use means for traversing the huge amounts of nodes and relations required to represent large and complex software systems.

The identified *disadvantages* concern, first, the *limited usefulness of standard database frontends* for end users. The issue with highly generic clients such as the Neo4j browser and similar tools is not a limitation in their functionality. On the contrary, they provide too many options. Custom interfaces built for end users offer only a fraction of their functionality, but they are meaningful in context of a specific usage scenario. Second, graph databases provide *no support for time series data*. Although this is natural consequence of the specialization of graph databases, there is nevertheless the need to represent time-related aspects in all kind of data produced in software development processes.

In future we expect to see a rising number of projects using graph databases for source code analysis and related software engineering tasks. As contribution we plan to investigate ways to combine storage approaches specialized for graph and time series data for building a new tool and service infrastructure.

Acknowledgements. The research reported in this paper was supported by the Austrian Ministry for Transport, Innovation and Technology, the Federal Ministry for Digital and Economic Affairs, and the Province of Upper Austria in the frame of the COMET center SCCH.

References

1. Alves, T.L., Hage, J., Rademaker, P.: A comparative study of code query technologies. In: 11th IEEE International Working Conference on Source Code Analysis and Manipulation (SCAM) 2011, pp. 145–154. IEEE (2011)
2. Angerer, F., Prähofer, H., Ramler, R., Grillenberger, F.: Points-to analysis of IEC 61131–3 programs: Implementation and application. In: IEEE 18th Conference on Emerging Technologies & Factory Automation (ETFA) 2013, pp. 1–8. IEEE (2013)
3. Angles, R.: A comparison of current graph database models. In: IEEE 28th International Conference on Data Engineering Workshops (ICDEW) 2012. pp. 171–177. IEEE (2012)
4. Angles, R., Gutierrez, C.: Survey of graph database models. ACM Comput. Surv. (CSUR) **40**(1), 1 (2008)
5. Buchgeher, G., Ernstbrunner, C., Ramler, R., Lusser, M.: Towards tool-support for test case selection in manual regression testing. In: IEEE Sixth International Conference on Software Testing, Verification and Validation Workshops (ICSTW) 2013, pp. 74–79. IEEE (2013)
6. Buchgeher, G., Weinreich, R., Huber, H.: A platform for the automated provisioning of architecture information for large-scale service-oriented software systems. In: European Conference on Software Architecture. Springer (2018) (to appear)
7. Fleck, G., Kirchmayr, W., Moser, M., Nocke, L., Pichler, J., Tober, R., Witlatschil, M.: Experience report on building ASTM based tools for multi-language reverse engineering. In:IEEE 23rd International Conference on Software Analysis, Evolution, and Reengineering (SANER) 2016, vol. 1, pp. 683–687. IEEE (2016)
8. Goonetilleke, O., Meibusch, D., Barham, B.: Graph data management of evolving dependency graphs for multi-versioned codebases. In: IEEE International Conference on Software Maintenance and Evolution (ICSME) 2017, pp. 574–583. IEEE (2017)
9. Hawes, N., Barham, B., Cifuentes, C.: Frappé: Querying the Linux kernel dependency graph. In: Proceedings of the GRADES 2015, p. 4. ACM (2015)
10. Ikkink, H.K.: Gradle Dependency Management. Packt Publishing, Birmingham (2015)
11. John, K.H., Tiegelkamp, M.: IEC 61131–3: Programming Industrial Automation Systems. Concepts and Programming Languages, Requirements for Programming Systems Decision-making Aids. Springer, Heidelberg (2010). https://doi.org/10.1007/978-3-642-12015-2
12. Juergens, E., Hummel, B., Deissenboeck, F., Feilkas, M., Schlogel, C., Wubbeke, A.: Regression test selection of manual system tests in practice. In: 15th European Conference on Software Maintenance and Reengineering, pp. 309–312, March 2011
13. Passos, L., Terra, R., Valente, M.T., Diniz, R., das Mendonca, N.C.: Static architecture-conformance checking: an illustrative overview. IEEE Softw. **27**(5), 82–89 (2010)
14. Pawlak, R., Monperrus, M., Petitprez, N., Noguera, C., Seinturier, L.: SPOON: A library for implementing analyses and transformations of Java source code. Softw. Pract. Exp. **46**(9), 1155–1179 (2015)

15. Prähofer, H., Angerer, F., Ramler, R., Grillenberger, F.: Static code analysis of iec 61131–3 programs: Comprehensive tool support and experiences from large-scale industrial application. IEEE Trans. Ind. Inform. **13**(1), 37–47 (2017)
16. Prähofer, H., Angerer, F., Ramler, R., Lacheiner, H., Grillenberger, F.: Opportunities and challenges of static code analysis of iec 61131–3 programs. In: IEEE 17th Conference on Emerging Technologies & Factory Automation (ETFA), pp. 1–8. IEEE (2012)
17. Ramler, R., Salomon, C., Buchgeher, G., Lusser, M.: Tool support for change-based regression testing: an industry experience report. In: Winkler, D., Biffl, S., Bergsmann, J. (eds.) SWQD 2017. LNBIP, vol. 269, pp. 133–152. Springer, Cham (2017). https://doi.org/10.1007/978-3-319-49421-0_10
18. Robinson, I., Webber, J., Eifrem, E.: Graph Databases: New Opportunities for Connected Data. O'Reilly. Media Inc., Sebastopol (2015)
19. Runeson, P., Host, M., Rainer, A., Regnell, B.: Case Study Research in Software Engineering. Guidelines and Examples. Wiley, Hoboken (2012)
20. Thaller, H.: Probabilistic Software Modeling, Jun 2018. arXiv:1806.08942 [cs]
21. Urma, R.G., Mycroft, A.: Source-code queries with graph databases-with application to programming language usage and evolution. Sci. Comput. Program. **97**, 127–134 (2015)
22. Yamaguchi, F., Golde, N., Arp, D., Rieck, K.: Modeling and discovering vulnerabilities with code property graphs. In: IEEE Symposium on Security and Privacy (SP), pp. 590–604. IEEE (2014)
23. Yoo, S., Harman, M.: Regression testing minimization, selection and prioritization: a survey. Softw. Test. Verif. Reliab. **22**(2), 67–120 (2012)
24. Zhang, T., Pan, M., Zhao, J., Yu, Y., Li, X.: An open framework for semantic code queries on heterogeneous repositories. In: International Symposium on Theoretical Aspects of Software Engineering (TASE), pp. 39–46. IEEE (2015)

Software Maintenance

Evaluating Maintainability Prejudices with a Large-Scale Study of Open-Source Projects

Tobias Roehm[1](✉), Daniel Veihelmann[1](✉), Stefan Wagner[2](✉) (iD),
and Elmar Juergens[1](✉)

[1] CQSE GmbH, Munich, Germany
{roehm,veihelmann,juergens}@cqse.eu
[2] University of Stuttgart, Stuttgart, Germany
stefan.wagner@iste.uni-stuttgart.de

Abstract. In software engineering, relying on experience can render maintainability expertise into prejudice over time. For example, based on their own experience, some consider JavaScript as inelegant language and hence of lowest maintainability. Such prejudice should not guide decisions without prior empirical validation.

Hence, we formulated 10 hypotheses about maintainability based on prejudices and test them in a large set of open-source projects (6,897 GitHub repositories, 402 million lines, 5 programming languages). We operationalize maintainability with five static analysis metrics.

We found that JavaScript code is not worse than other code, Java code shows higher maintainability than C# code and C code has longer methods than other code. The quality of interface documentation is better in Java code than in other code. Code developed by teams is not of higher and large code bases not of lower maintainability. Projects with high maintainability are not more popular or more often forked. Overall, most hypotheses are not supported by open-source data.

Keywords: Maintainability · Software quality
Programming language · Static analysis · Metrics
Open source · GitHub · Empirical study · Case study

1 Introduction

To implement a feature or fix a bug, software developers have to identify relevant code regions and comprehend them. As program comprehension is part of many maintenance tasks, developers can spend 50–70% of their time on it [15,28]. Source code with high quality makes it easier for developers to comprehend it [26]. Hence, developers working with highly maintainable code can fix bugs faster, implement features more rapidly, and spend less effort compared to developers working with low-quality code.

© Springer Nature Switzerland AG 2019
D. Winkler et al. (Eds.): SWQD 2019, LNBIP 338, pp. 151–171, 2019.
https://doi.org/10.1007/978-3-030-05767-1_10

Due to this importance of maintainability, developers form their own "theories" of the interrelations of programming languages, team characteristics or code size with maintainability based on their daily experiences. By cumulating and discussing such experiences with others, they can become "prejudices". Such prejudices will then be the basis for decisions in projects. Therefore, empirical research should evaluate whether such prejudices are really supported by facts and data. Yet, there are few empirical studies on these subjects.

To help close this gap, we contribute a large-scale study about ten hypotheses derived from our practical experience with prejudices related to maintainability. We investigate maintainability in relation to programming languages, project size and project popularity. We operationalize the abstract concept of maintainability by analyzing open-source code with respect to five static analysis metrics: clone coverage, too long files, too long methods, nesting depth and comment incompleteness. All these metrics identify code smells which increase the effort for developers during program comprehension. While they cannot cover maintainability completely, based on existing studies and our consulting experience, they are good indicators for maintainability.

We chose GitHub as a source of open-source code, randomly selected repositories, downloaded their code, excluded irrelevant code automatically and performed static analysis. We considered GitHub repositories with code written in C, C#, C++, Java, or JavaScript. We chose these languages because (1) they are all similar from a syntactical standpoint ("C-family"), which makes our used metrics better comparable, and (2) our used analysis tool covers them well. Overall, our data set contains 6,897 repositories containing 402 million source lines of code.[1]

This paper complements other empirical studies on quality, especially the studies by Ray et al. [32,33] and Bissyandé et al. [9]. They operationalize quality focusing on the number of bug fixing commits or the number of issues. While faults are an interesting aspect of quality, we found that our set of static code metrics represent the maintainability side.

The contribution of this paper is a large-scale study of maintainability in open-source projects. The study investigates 10 prejudices formalized as statistical hypotheses. It covers the comparison of the maintainability of code in different languages overall as well as specific aspects of maintainability. Furthermore, we investigate the relationships of maintainability and the team and code size as well as the forks and popularity of open-source projects. To the best of our knowledge, this is the largest study of maintainability and the first large-scale study of maintainability in open-source projects operationalizing maintainability with a set of static analysis metrics. We provide a replication package.[2]

---

[1] "Lines of code" denotes all lines in a file or method, "source lines of code" all lines while ignoring empty lines and comments.

[2] See https://github.com/Dan1ve/MSR17CodeQualityOnGitHub.

2   Related Work

Ray et al. [32,33] present a similar study on code quality of GitHub code. They investigate the effect of programming languages and their properties as well as the impact of application domains on code quality. In contrast to this study, they operationalize code quality by the number of bug fix commits. Bissyandé et al. [9] present another similar study on software quality of GitHub repositories. They investigate the impact of programming languages on project success, code quality, and team size. In contrast to this study, they measure code quality by the number of issue reports. We offer the complementary view of static analysis.

Static analysis has been used by other researchers to investigate the quality of open-source code. But most of that research considers few software applications or few programming languages. Samoladas et al. [36] and Stamelos et al. [38] present studies on code quality of open-source code. Norick et al. [30] present a study on open-source code, investigating the impact of team size on code quality. All three papers also use static analysis to measure code quality, they use different metrics, which we consider less suitable for maintainability. Furthermore, they do not investigate the impact of programming language or other factors on quality. Ahmed, Ghorashi and Jensen [4] investigate the code quality of open-source code by examining the correlation between code smells and project characteristics. They do not investigate the impact of programming language and use different static analysis metrics.

All these studies either used outdated and strongly criticised metrics such as the Halstead metrics, the Maintainability Index or more detailed bug pattern analysis. We concentrated on metrics that are automatically collectable, have been proven in practice to be good indicators for quality and are measurable across languages [18,31,40]. Only Koschke and Bazrafshan [25] also investigate cloning in their study on clone rates in code written in C and C++. Yet, they focus only on programming languages and cloning.

Several studies investigated aspects of software quality. Kochhar, Wijedasa and Lo [24] present a study on code quality of GitHub code which examines the impact of language co-use on code quality. Bird et al. [7] did a study on software quality of industry code which investigates the influence of distributed development on software quality. Bird et al. [8] also present a study on software quality of industry code which studies the impact of code ownership on software quality. Nagappan, Murphy and Basili [29] examine software quality of industry software by investigating the effect of organizational structure on software quality. All these studies consider different aspects of software quality than this study and operationalize quality differently.

For a more detailed overview of code quality measurement of open-source code we refer to Ruiz and Robinson [34] and Spinellis et al. [37]. Beller et al. [6] present a study on static analysis tools on GitHub. While they focus on the usage of static analysis, we take advantage of static analysis results as an operationalization of code quality.

3   Study Design

3.1   Research Questions

The focus of this study is prejudices on maintainability. We investigate the following two research questions:

RQ1: How does the programming language affect maintainability? One major area of prejudices is about the impact of the programming language on maintainability. We examine whether code written in one programming language differs in quality from code written in another programming language. We formulate six hypotheses about potential relationships between programming language and maintainability.

RQ2: How do non-language aspects influence or are influenced by maintainability? In addition to the programming language, many other aspects are often seen as factors that might influence maintainability. This study investigates further factors by using the meta data of GitHub repositories and relating them to maintainability metrics. The following aspects form four more hypotheses to be tested: code base size, team size, individual vs. team code, development activity and repository popularity.

3.2   Hypotheses Formalizing Prejudices

To make prejudices analyzable in an empirical study, we formulated ten hypotheses about maintainability before performing data collection and analysis (cf. Table 1). This avoids cherry-picking obvious results from the dataset and thereby "overfitting" to the studied dataset [13]. Our hypotheses can be divided in two categories: assumptions about the impact of the programming language on maintainability[3] (cf. RQ1) and hypotheses about the influence of other aspects on maintainability (cf. RQ2). The hypotheses consider the languages C, C++, C#, Java, and JavaScript.

The motivation behind H1 and H4 is the fact that C is not an object-oriented language. Hence, in situations where developers of object-oriented languages can use inheritance, developers of C code probably have to duplicate the code. H2 was derived from the fact that Java and C# are very similar languages. The idea behind H3 is that JavaScript code might contain anonymous callback functions more frequently, which might lead to deeper nested code. Since documentation frameworks like JavaDoc are available for all of the studied languages, we assume that there is no difference in this regard (H5). The motivation behind H6 is the assumption that JavaScript development often has a rapid development pace, making it challenging to produce high-quality code. H7 is based on the prejudice that team members push each other to develop high-quality code and high-quality code is necessary for collective code ownership. The motivation

---

[3] Apart from personal experience and discussions based on blog posts such as http://live.julik.nl/2013/05/javascript-is-shit.

behind H8 is the assumption that small code bases can keep higher maintainability standards more easily than large code bases. The idea behind H9 is the assumption that developers like to work with high-quality code bases and, hence, such repositories have more forks.

Table 1. Overview of hypotheses "other languages" and "all languages" refers to the set (C, C++, C#, Java, JavaScript), "very long" etc. refers to the static analysis metrics from Table 2

Hypotheses on languages	
H1	C code has more code duplication than code written in other languages
H2	Code written in Java and C# has no differences regarding maintainability
H3	JavaScript code is more deeply nested than code written in other languages
H4	C code has more very long methods than code written in other languages
H5	The quality of interface documentation is similar for all languages
H6	JavaScript code has the lowest maintainability among all languages
Hypotheses on project size	
H7	Code developed by a team has a better quality than code developed by an individual
H8	Large code bases have a lower quality than small code bases
Hypotheses on project popularity	
H9	Repositories with high maintainability have more forks than repositories with low maintainability
H10	Repositories with high maintainability are more popular than repositories with low maintainability

3.3   Object Selection

This study uses GitHub [2] as source of open-source code because the platform hosts a huge number of repositories and it provides infrastructure for selecting and downloading code (see Gousios [17] and the GitHub API [3]). We used the GHTorrent data set [17] (Version 2016-03-16) to pre-select relevant GitHub repositories. GHTorrent is a repository of GitHub meta data.

Inclusion and Exclusion Criteria. We defined inclusion and exclusion criteria that a GitHub repository has to fulfill to be relevant for this study. The goal of these criteria is to maximize the validity of the results. Some criteria are based on advice by Kalliamvakou et al. [23]. We applied the following criteria:

Programming Language: One of the repository's languages has to be C, C++, C#, Java, or JavaScript. We focus on these languages because they are all syntactically similar ("C-family") and, hence, the metrics are more likely to be comparable across languages, the used code analysers support these languages, and we reuse preliminary work when excluding irrelevant code (cf. Sect. 3.4).

Minimum Size of Code Base: The code base must have at least 10,000 lines of code. This criterion is used to exclude small repositories which might bias the results and are likely to be dummy repositories.

No Fork or Mirror: A repository must not be a fork or mirror of another repository. This criterion is used to concentrate on the main repositories and avoid analyzing the same code base multiple times.

Availability of Description: The repository must have a readme file and/or a GitHub description. This criterion is used to filter out dummy repositories.

Maximum Size of Code Base: The size of the code base per language must not exceed 215 MB. This criterion is used to exclude large repositories which contain the same code multiple times, e.g. in different versions. 99% of repositories in the GHTorrent dataset are below this threshold and an empirical investigation (conducted by two authors as part of this study) showed that 75% of repositories exceeding this threshold contain the same code multiple times.

Maximum Clone Coverage: The clone coverage of a repository must be smaller than 75%. When manually analyzing code bases with high clone coverage, we found that the majority of them contained the same application multiple times. Empirical evaluation of different threshold values revealed that a threshold of 75% is a good compromise between considering as many repositories as possible and excluding irrelevant repositories.

When applicable, these criteria were applied to the GHTorrent data set. The criteria "Minimum Size of Code Base" and "Maximum Clone Coverage" were applied after static analysis because they require the corresponding results. Only repositories that fulfill all criteria were added to the final data set and used in further analysis. The final data set consists of 6,897 repositories containing 402 million source lines of code.

Random Sampling. The GitHub repositories considered in the study were selected randomly. To perform this step, the list of GitHub repositories matching the criteria was ordered randomly and repositories were downloaded starting at the top of the list.

3.4   Data Collection Procedures

After selecting the GitHub repositories, we downloaded their code and removed generated code, test code and library code to focus the analysis on production code and improve comparability of results.

Download via GitHub API. The code of selected GitHub repositories was downloaded using the GitHub API [3]. In addition to code, we retrieved meta data of repositories like the number of committers or the number of stars. This meta data is used to investigate the impact of non-language aspects on maintainability (cf. RQ2).

Exclusion of Irrelevant Code. Code generated by tools distorts the results of static analysis. This is especially true for clone detection as generated code often follows a pattern which is likely to be classified as a clone. Hence, we exclude generated code. Test code is code executed to verify the correctness of an application [5]. Despite its importance, we exclude test code to achieve better comparability between repositories and because developers might not apply high quality standards to it (c.f. Steidl and Deissenboeck [39]). When manually analyzing a sample of GitHub repositories, we found that repositories often contain library code. Library code denotes code that is developed by a third party and was copied into a repository, probably for reuse purposes. This is common for JavaScript repositories where library code is often included as source files and not as binaries. We exclude library code since we solely focus on the primary repository code.

We used four mechanisms to exclude irrelevant code:

Comment exclusion uses code comments that indicate that a file is generated or part of a library, e.g. "@license AngularJS v1.0.7 (c)". We use a list of 2,247 exclusion comments assembled by Hoenick [20]. According to Hoenick [20], this approach excludes 97% of generated code.

Path exclusion is based on file system paths which indicate that code files in a directory are generated, test code or library code, e.g. "**/generated/**". We use a list of 58 exclusion paths assembled by Hoenick [20].

Import exclusion exploits import statements of popular test frameworks such as JUnit. We use a list of 10 test framework imports assembled by Hoenick. According to him, this approach excludes 90% of test code.

File name exclusion is based on the file name frequency of popular library files. We counted the frequency of file names in all downloaded repositories, manually reviewed the 200 most frequent file names, extracted a list of 60 library files, and excluded the corresponding files. Furthermore, we ignore minified JavaScript – code which was automatically shrunk to reduce file size and thus looks significantly different than the original code – by its file suffixes, e.g. "min.js". These efforts aim at excluding library code as precisely as possible. A manual evaluation indicated that we got rid of most library code.

3.5   Operationalization of Maintainability

The operationalization of software quality in general and also maintainability in particular has not been solved satisfyingly in general. Several quality model approaches have aimed at systematically deriving good indicators [19,35,41]. Yet, it is difficult to cover all aspects of maintainability. We follow here our proposal of an activity-based maintainability model [12] and focus on statically measurable indicators to be feasible for our large-scale study. We select static metrics which we expect to have an impact on the main maintenance-related activity *code comprehension* (cf. Table 2): clone coverage, too long files, too long methods, nesting depth and comment incompleteness. Furthermore, we chose these metrics because they are easy to understand and improve, they are language-independent, they have been found to be suitable for making solid statements about software maintainability [31] and they are used in practice [18, 40].

Table 2. Overview of static analysis metrics unit of all metrics is percentage where higher values indicate lower quality.

Metric	Definition
Clone coverage	The fraction of source lines in the code base which are part of at least one (type 2) clone
Comment incompleteness	The fraction of public classes, types, methods, procedures, and attributes which are not documented by a comment
Too long files	The fraction of source lines in the code base which are located in files exceeding 750 source lines
Too long methods	The fraction of source lines in the code base which are located in methods exceeding 75 source lines
Nesting depth	The fraction of source lines in the code base which are located in methods with at least one line exceeding nesting depth 5

The metric "clone coverage" [40] indicates the fraction of the code base which is part of at least one clone. If the value is high, this means that developers frequently encounter duplicated code. Code clones unnecessarily increase a code base. Furthermore, faults fixed in one clone instance can remain present in other clone instances and inconsistent clones likely introduce bugs [21]. The metric "too long files" [40] identifies the fraction of the code base which is located in long files. Long files are often difficult to comprehend as one has to consider a large fragment of code. In addition, long files might be a hint for bad modularization.

The metric "too long methods" [40] identifies the fraction of the code base which is located in long methods. Long methods are difficult for developers to comprehend because they have to consider much code. Furthermore, long methods might be an indicator for bad modularization. The metric "nesting depth" [40] identifies the fraction of the code base which is located in methods which are deeply nested. These are difficult to comprehend because each condition "controlling" a nested statement has to be taken into consideration to tell when the statement is executed.

Finally, metric "comment incompleteness" [18] identifies code entities like methods, classes, or attributes, which lack any kind of explanatory comment. Missing documentation makes it expensive for developers to comprehend what a code entity does and how it can be reused. We make two restrictions here: we consider only public code entities and we ignore trivial getter/setter methods as well as overriding methods. We only regard public code entities because they are open for reuse and hence we expect them to be documented. Ignoring getter and setter methods accommodates the fact that these methods are often too trivial to document. We ignore overriding methods because usually the documentation of the overridden method is sufficient.

All of these metrics use percentage values as unit of measurement where high percentage values indicate low maintainability. This makes it easier to interpret and compare metric values.

3.6   Analysis Procedures

We performed three types of analysis: static analysis to calculate metric values, descriptive statistics for an overview of the data and inferential statistics to test hypotheses. The details of these analyses are described in the following paragraphs. All statistical analyses were performed with R.

Static Analysis. We use the open-source tool ConQAT [1,11] to calculate static analysis metrics for each GitHub repository after download and exclusion of irrelevant code. We used the following static analysis parameters: For the metric "clone coverage", we consider clones that consist of ten or more consecutive statements. In addition to identical fragments of source code, we consider clones that contain simple modifications such as variable renamings (i.e. type 2 clones). For the metric "too long files", we consider source lines in files with more than 750 source lines of code in the percentage value, which is less strict than e.g. Martin [26] who advocates file size of less than 500 lines. For the metric "too long methods", we consider source lines in methods with more than 75 source lines of code in the percentage value, which is less strict than e.g. Martin [26] who advocates method with less than 20 lines. While it might look inappropriate to use the same threshold values for different languages on a first glance, we argue that – given the rather lenient threshold values where a method already spans several screens – the constraints of developers' working memory are the dominating factor [27], independent of the language.

For the metric "nesting depth", we consider code lines in methods which have at least one statement with nesting depth 5 or deeper in the percentage value. Again, this is less strict than Martin [26] who advocates nesting depths below 2. And finally for the metric "comment incompleteness", we consider all public types, methods, functions, procedures, properties, attributes and declarations, but we exclude simple getter methods, setter methods and override methods in the percentage value. This is in accordance with respective guidelines [16,18]. We did not evaluate comment incompleteness for JavaScript code because this analysis is not supported by ConQAT. All configuration details can also be found in a configuration file in the replication package.

Statistical Analysis. To aggregate results from individual code bases to groups of code bases and compare results of different groups, we used basic statistics like minimum, maximum, or median. Because no data attribute exhibits a normal distribution and variances differ, we report median instead of mean and use corresponding statistical procedures. Nevertheless, we use MANOVA analyses for first tests if the null hypotheses could be rejected at all in cases where quality overall, and hence all quality metrics, is involved. We believe this is a valid approach, because for more detailed comparisons, we then choose more robust non-parametric methods. Yet, if a parametric approach finds no significant difference, it is not necessary to investigate further.

We studied ten hypotheses about maintainability (cf. Table 1). Because they either formulate a hypothesis about a single quality metric or quality overall. For single quality metrics, we use the Kruskal test first to see if there are any differences at all. To investigate which group is significantly different from another, we applied a (pairwise) Mann–Whitney U test (also known as Wilcoxon rank sum test, see Kabacoff [22]). In the case of pairwise tests, probability adjustment according to Holm is used. This non-parametric test can be used for two independent groups that are not normally distributed and with different group sizes. In cases where quality overall is part of a hypothesis, we use a MANOVA first to test whether there is a difference for any quality metric. In case there is a difference, we use single ANOVA tests to see which quality metrics are significantly different. For those, we then use the non-parametric Mann-Whitney U test for pairwise comparisons. For H8, we employ Pearson's coefficient to quantify the relationship between the size of the code bases with the quality metrics. We use a significance level of $p < 0.01$. We use Cohen's d for effect sizes and Cliff's delta or Pearson's correlation coefficient as alternative where necessary.

3.7   Validity Procedures

We employed the following procedures to maximize the validity of the results. First, we refined the inclusion and exclusion criteria several times to filter out GitHub repositories which might distort the results (cf. Sect. 3.3). Second, we used only data for which we are confident of their quality and validity. For instance, we refrained from analysing maintainability with the number of open issues, number of pull request or release count. While these would be interesting to analyze, only a fraction of GitHub repositories uses these GitHub features [23]. Hence, these data attributes are probably not valid and would lead to meaningless results. Third, we manually browsed through a sample of about 50 repositories to see what kinds of artefacts are present. This analysis led to the detection and exclusion of library code and minified JavaScript code. Fourth, we manually verified the static analysis results of a sample of roughly 30 repositories. Fifth, we manually analyzed a sample of approx. 90 repositories with exceptionally high or low metric values. For repositories with very high clone coverage, we found that this is often caused by multiple project copies within one repository. Thus, we established a maximum value of 75% for clone coverage. Sixth, the static analysis was mainly performed by one author and the results were reviewed by another author for validity and coherence. Seventh, we considered a large sample of repositories—more than 600 per programming language—in the analysis. Finally, we use a conservative significance level for the statistical test ($\alpha = 0.01$).

3.8 Study Objects

Table 3 provides an overview of studied GitHub repositories. Overall, about 1 million repositories in the GHTorrent data set fulfilled the selection criteria. After download and code exclusions, our data set consisted of 6,897 repositories containing 402 million source lines of code overall. Only repositories that fulfill all criteria (cf. Sect. 3.3) were added to this data set. The size of the repositories varies from 991 SLoC to 1.3 m SLoC with a median size of 20 k SLoC (please note that we put the minimum size constraint on LoC and not SLoC). The number of repositories per language varies because we downloaded repositories in a round robin fashion but excluded already downloaded repositories when their size fell below 10 kLoC after code exclusions. About half of the repositories (3,434) were individual repositories, i.e. repositories with just one committer, while the other half (3,463) were team repositories. The number of commits varied from 1 to 507,000 with a median of 40 commits. The most forked repository had 8,790 forks while most repositories were not forked at all. Similarly, the most popular repository had 19,200 stars while most repositories had no stars.

Table 3. Overview of study subjects/GitHub repositories k = 1,000, m = 1,000,000, Format of multi-value cells: Median (Min-Max)

Lang.	Relev. repos	Used repos	Used SLoC	Size (SLoC)	#committer	#commits	#forks	#stars
C	139 k	2,072	138 m	25 k (2 k–939 k)	2 (1–835)	37 (1–114 k)	0 (0–6.7 k)	0 (0–19.2 k)
C++	141 k	2,035	173 m	25 k (2 k–1.2 m)	2 (1–15 k)	46 (1–507 k)	0 (0–8.7 k)	0 (0–15.8 k)
C#	70 k	716	22 m	15 k (5 k–904 k)	2 (1–110)	55 (1–27 k)	1 (0–1.6 k)	0 (0–8.2 k)
Java	203 k	978	31 m	14 k (1 k–710 k)	2 (1–132)	53 (1–22 k)	0 (0–2.1 k)	0 (0–3.5 k)
JS	496 k	1,096	37 m	22 k (4 k–628 k)	1 (1–325)	25 (1–119 k)	0 (0–1.9 k)	0 (0–5.7 k)
All	1.1 m	6,897	402 m	20 k (1 k–1.2 m)	2 (1–15 k)	40 (1–507 k)	0 (0–8.7 k)	0 (0–19.2 k)

4 Study Results

This section presents study results. It is structured according to the research questions and summarizes the findings in boxes.

4.1 General Descriptive Statistics

Table 4 presents descriptive statistics for the quality metrics of the analysed repositories. It shows median values where *higher* percentage values indicate *lower* quality. Clone coverage ranges between 7% and 11%, indicating that on average about 1/10 of the code is part of at least one clone. There are no big differences between programming languages. Comment incompleteness ranges between 60% and 75%, meaning that on average almost 3/4 of public code entities are not commented. Java code exhibits notably higher quality in that respect than code written in C, C++ or C#. Please note that this metric was not computed for JavaScript repositories.

The median of the metric "too long files" is 37%, indicating that roughly one-third of the code is located in files which are longer than 750 source lines of code. This metric varies a lot between programming languages, namely from 10% (Java) to 70% (JavaScript). The median of the metric "too long methods" is 18%, indicating that on average one-fifth of the code is placed in methods whose length exceed 75 source lines of code. Metric values for programming languages vary a lot from 3% (JavaScript) to 31% (C). Nesting depth ranges between 1% and 5%, indicating that on average very few code is located in deeply nested methods. We summarize the descriptive findings in the following statements:

- Only a small fraction of code bases is part of a clone or located in deeply nested methods. For these metrics, there is no strong difference between C, C++, C#, Java and JavaScript code.
- 3/4 of public code entities are not documented by a comment. Java code is documented more completely than code written in C, C++, or C#.
- 1/3 of the code is located in long files. This value heavily varies between programming languages, ranging from 9% for Java code to 70% for JavaScript code.
- 1/5 of the code is located in long methods. This value varies between programming languages, ranging from 3% for JavaScript code to 30% for C code.

Table 4. Overview of metric results, median values, higher % values indicate lower quality, "–": No data

Language	Clone coverage	Comment incompleteness	File size	Method length	Nesting depth
C	7%	72%	48%	31%	5%
C++	8%	74%	36%	21%	4%
C#	11%	75%	16%	13%	3%
Java	9%	60%	10%	10%	2%
JavaScript	9%	–	70%	3%	1%
All	8%	72%	37%	18%	3%

4.2 How Does the Programming Language Affect Maintainability (RQ1)?

H1: C code has more code duplication than code written in other languages. Table 4 shows the median clone coverage values by language. These figures already suggest that there is only little difference between C-projects and the ones in other languages. The overall null hypothesis that there is no difference between the code duplication in code of different languages has to be rejected however (p-value < 0.0001). Hence, we can look in more detail into the comparison of C code against other code. The pairwise comparisons show that the null hypotheses that there is no difference in clone coverage between C code and the respective other languages cannot be rejected (p-value of 1 for all comparisons, d between 0.04 and 0.22).

> C code has no higher clone coverage than code written in C++, C#, Java, or JavaScript.

H2: Code written in C# and Java has no differences regarding maintainability. Here, we only analysed the data from C# and Java projects. The MANOVA analysis showed that we have to reject the null hypothesis that there is no difference in the quality of C# and Java code (p-value < 0.0001). In the ANOVA analyses of single metrics, we found only in nesting depth that there was no significant difference (p-value = 0.38, d = 0.05). In the Wilcoxon tests, significant differences are in clone coverage (p-value = 0.0006, d = 0.19), large files (p-value < 0.0001, d = 0.34), large methods (p-value < 0.0001, d = 0.22) and comment completeness (p-value < 0.0001). Hence, we have to reject the hypothesis that there is no difference in quality between C# and Java code apart from their nesting depth. This also fits to the median values in Table 4 which show better values for Java then for C# for all metrics. Yet, the effect sizes are small.

> Java code shows better maintainability than C# code.

H3: JavaScript code is more deeply nested than code written in other languages. The Kruskal-Wallis test showed that we need to reject the null hypotheses that there is no difference between the deep nesting of code in different programming languages (p-value < 0.0001). Hence, we can go beyond the omnibus hypothesis and look more closely on JavaScript. The pairwise comparisons of the Wilcoxon test showed that we cannot reject the hypothesis that there is no difference in nesting depth between JavaScript and any of the other four language (p-value = 1 for all languages, d between 0.01 and 0.34). In fact, the median nesting depth is lower than in all other languages.

> JavaScript code does not differ in deep nesting from code written in C, C++, C#, or Java.

H4: C code has more very long methods than code written in other languages. The Kruskal-Wallis test showed that the null hypothesis that there is no difference in the number of long methods between code in different languages has to be rejected (p-value < 0.0001). Hence, we can look further in the specific position of C. All pairwise Wilcoxon tests showed that the null hypotheses has to be rejected (p-value < 0.0001 for all languages, d = 0.44 for C++, d = 0.73 for C#, d = 0.94 for Java, d = 0.99 for JavaScript). We have to accept the alternative hypothesis that C code has more very long methods than code written in other languages.

> C code has longer methods than code written in C++, C#, Java, or JavaScript.

H5: The quality of interface documentation is similar for all languages.
Since ConQAT does not support the detection of JavaScript documentation, we limited the scope of this analysis to the four remaining languages. The Kruskal-Wallis test showed that the null hypothesis that there is no difference in the quality of interface documentation across languages has to be rejected (p-value < 0.0001). A further analysis using pairwise Wilcoxon tests showed statistically significant differences only between Java and C ($\delta = 0.25$), C++ ($\delta = 0.25$) and C# ($\delta = 0.22$, p-values all < 0.0001). There is no statistically significant difference between C, C++, C# and JavaScript as well as between Java and JavaScript (all p-values = 1, δs between 0.01 and 0.31). Hence, we have to reject the hypothesis that the quality of interface documentation is similar for all languages. Instead, we have support for a new hypothesis that the quality of interface documentation is better in Java code then in most other code.

> The interface documentation of Java code is better than for code written in C, C++, and C# and there is no difference between the three latter languages.

H6: JavaScript code has the lowest maintainability among all languages. The null hypothesis that there is no difference in maintainability among code bases written in different languages has to be rejected. The MANOVA analysis gave a p-value smaller than 0.0001. A further look into the single ANOVA analyses showed that this holds for all single used quality metrics. Hence, we analyzed the pairwise comparisons with JavaScript using Wilcoxon tests. We analyzed the nesting depth already in H3 and found no difference. We also already investigated comment completeness in H5 and found no difference. The further analysis showed no significant difference in clone coverage (C: p-value = 0.03, d = 0.29, C++: p-value = 0.35, d=0.26, C#: p-value = 1, d = 0.05 and Java: p-value = 1, d = 0.22). For large files, JavaScript is significantly worse than all other languages with medium to large effect sizes (d = 0.60 for C, d = 1.04 for C++, d = 1.54 for C# and d = 1.99 for Java, p-values < 0.0001 for all languages). Finally, for long methods, there is no statistically significant difference (p-value = 1 for all languages, d between 0.12 and 0.91). The large effect sizes here are because the JavaScript tends to have the lowest number of too long methods. Based on this, with only one quality metric in which JavaScript is worst, we decided to reject the hypothesis that JavaScript code has the lowest maintainability in all analyzed languages. Instead, we adopt the new hypothesis that there is no overall difference in quality of code written in the analysed languages.

> Maintainability of JavaScript code is *not* lower compared to code written in C, C++, C#, or Java.

4.3   Which Non-language Aspects Influence or Are Influenced by Maintainability (RQ2)?

H7: Code developed by a team has better quality than code developed by an individual. The null hypotheses that there is no difference in the quality of code developed by different numbers of contributors could not be rejected. The MANOVA analysis gave a p-value of 0.26. Hence, we cannot accept H7. Code developed in teams is not associated with higher maintainability.

> Code developed in teams does not have better quality then code developed by an individual.

H8: Large code bases have a lower quality than small code bases. The MANOVA analysis showed that the null hypothesis that there is no difference in quality of code bases of different sizes has to be rejected (p-value < 0.0001). Looking into the individual ANOVA analyses, only the metric "too long files" showed a difference. To investigate this in more detail, we calculated Pearson's product-moment correlation with correlation coefficient 0.1004 and a p-value < 0.0001. Hence, large code bases tend to have more very large files. Yet, there is only a difference for this one metric with a small effect size. Therefore, we propose that we cannot accept H8. Low maintainability is not more associated with larger code bases.

> Large code bases do not have worse maintainability then small code bases.

H9: Repositories with high maintainability have more forks than repositories with low maintainability. The null hypotheses that there is no difference in the number of forks in repositories with different qualities cannot be rejected. The ANOVA analysis gave p-values of 0.12 (clone coverage), 0.91 (nesting depth), 0.25 (large files), 0.97 (large methods) and 0.90 (comment completeness). Hence, we cannot accept H9. High maintainability is not associated with more forks.

> Repositories with high maintainability do not have more forks.

H10: Repositories with high maintainability are more popular than repositories with low maintainability. The null hypotheses that there is no difference in popularity in repositories with different qualities cannot be rejected. The ANOVA analysis gave p-values of 0.021 (clone coverage), 0.56 (nesting depth), 0.19 (large files), 0.84 (large methods) and 0.91 (comment completeness). Hence, we cannot accept H10. High maintainability of projects is not associated with more popularity.

> Repositories with high maintainability are not more popular.

5   Discussion

This section discusses study results, summarizes implications, and presents threats to validity.

5.1   Results Discussion

When analyzing the resulting metric values (cf. Table 4), the question arises whether they are "good" or "bad". As all metric values are percentages, they indicate the likelihood of encountering a code smell, e.g. a clone, when selecting an arbitrary line from the code base. The higher this likelihood, the more often developers will have to deal with such maintainability issues. The median values for clone coverage and nesting depth are low, indicating that open-source developers rarely have to struggle with clones or deeply-nested methods. The rather low clone coverage values for code written in C and C++ match results by Koschke and Bazrafshan [25].

In contrast, half of the C code and 2/3 of JavaScript code is located in long files, which implies that C and JavaScript developers have to cope with long files frequently. Finally, 72% of all public code entities in code bases written in C, C++, C# or Java are not documented. Hence, developers frequently have to read and understand those in detail, e.g. for review or reuse purposes, which costs time and productivity and could be avoided.

Our results show that Java code has on average the highest and C code the lowest maintainability. Apart from the programming language, there might be other reasons to explain this finding: differing education on and community support for maintainability, differing refactoring support by IDEs, or the use of static analysis tools. We are not able to investigate these aspects and their impact on maintainability and leave this for future work.

Overall, only a single hypothesis could be supported by our large sample of open-source repositories: C code has longer methods than code written in the other languages. As C is the only non-object-oriented language in our analysis, we can see this as indication that structuring code according to object-oriented principles helps in writing smaller methods. All other hypotheses related to programming languages could not be supported.

To further study the impact of programming languages on maintainability, we identified top repositories by intersecting the sets of the 25% best repositories for all five metrics. Likewise, we identified flop repositories. Interestingly, repositories from each language are among the top and flop repositories, indicating that is possible to write high-quality – but also low-quality – code in every language. Hence, we conclude that language has a small impact on maintainability.

This result is in agreement with Ray et al. [32,33] and Bissyandé et al. [9]. Summarizing, three ways of operationalizing quality – bug fix commits, the number of issues, and static analysis metrics – come to the same conclusion: The programming language has likely only a modest influence on maintainability.

Not one hypothesis on maintainability and development activity, repository popularity, code base size, or team size could be supported. These results contrast with related work which found that software quality is influenced by the size of the code base [14] or the number of developers [8]. But they are in accordance with Weyuker et al. [42] and Norick et al. [30], who found that the number of developers has no major impact on code quality. Additionally, they agree with Ahmed et al. [4] who found that code quality is not affected by code base size.

In contrast, Ray et al. [33] found a strong correlation between the number of commits and code quality. This difference can be explained that their operationalization of quality (the number of bug fix commits) grows proportionally with the number of commits while ours does not. Furthermore, they are similar to results by Corral et al. [10] who found that the code quality of Android apps has only a marginal impact on market success.

5.2   Implications for Researchers and Practitioners

Implications for Researchers. That only 1 of 10 hypotheses was accepted shows the importance of empirical research to test assumptions about maintainability. When comparing study results with related work, we found that software quality is operationalized differently in different studies, e.g. as number of bug fix commits, number of issues, number of post-release defects, number of pre-release defects, or static analysis results. Hence, we find it interesting to compare these quality measurements – e.g. study whether they are correlated or if results are stable when changing the operationalization – and suggest future work in this direction. Furthermore, researchers should study contradictions between results of different studies regarding relationships of non-language aspects with maintainability.

Implications for Practitioners. Most importantly, practitioners should take the results of this study to challenge their own conceptions about maintainability. One might argue that the hypotheses we formulate do not represent such prejudices well. Yet, we show that all such conceptions need to be empirically tested if they are used for project decisions.

Furthermore, practitioners can use the metric values presented in this paper as a reference when interpreting static analysis results from their own code base. If a metric value for an own code base is worse than the average, this demonstrates that it is easily possible to write better code and it might encourage practitioners to improve their code base.

Moreover, practitioners should investigate whether their own code base suffers from problems and consider taking countermeasures. C developers should especially look at comment incompleteness, file size, and method length. C++ developers should in particular regard comment incompleteness and file size. C# and Java developers should especially look at comment incompleteness. JavaScript developers should, in particular, be aware of file sizes.

5.3   Threats to Validity

As we considered a random sample of a huge size from GitHub as the de-facto standard for open-source hosting today, we are rather confident that the results generalize to open-source systems in the investigated languages.

As we randomly sampled repositories from GitHub, the majority of repositories is rather small [23] and this might bias the results. To address this threat, we used a minimum threshold of 10,000 lines of code for the size of a repository.

Before performing static analysis, we excluded irrelevant code automatically (cf. Sect. 3.4). Due to the heterogeneity of GitHub repositories, we might not have excluded all irrelevant code which might bias the results. To minimize this effect, we improved the approach developed by Hönick [20] and manually verified the absence of irrelevant code in a random sample.

We did not discriminate between formatting styles when calculating the sizes of files and methods. Formatting styles denote whether opening and closing brackets are placed on separate lines. This fact might bias results to the disadvantage of C# code where brackets are usually put on separate lines. To address this threat, we chose high threshold values for size metrics.

When analyzing comment incompleteness, we targeted public code entities. While this concept is rather clear for code written in C#, Java, and JavaScript (because the languages provide visibility features), it is not so clear for code written in C and C++. For C, we considered all function definitions in header files. For C++, we considered the definitions of classes, methods and attributes in header files. This operationalization might bias the results when developers document code entities outside header files.

6   Conclusion

This paper presented a large-scale empirical study on prejudices about maintainability that we evaluated on open-source code bases. We used a random sample of 6,897 GitHub repositories containing 402 million lines of code written in C, C++, C#, Java and JavaScript. We automatically excluded irrelevant code and used static analysis to determine the maintainability of each code base. Based on this information, we investigated the impact of programming languages and other factors on maintainability. We provide all information necessary to replicate the study on GitHub. In agreement with related studies, we found that the programming language has only a modest impact on maintainability. In addition, we found that there is no significant relationship between maintainability and development activity, repository popularity, code base size and team size. This indicates that these factors and the programming language are no decisive factors regarding maintainability.

Future work should investigate first, what reasons and motivations are behind the results and elicit best practices for maintainability. To this end, we plan to compare top and flop GitHub repositories and interview developers. Second, it should evaluate the effects of code base size on the results. Third, it should consider more languages and more unproven assumptions. Fourth, it should study differences between open-source and closed-source code. Fifth, it should compare different operationalizations of maintainability.

References

1. ConQAT Homepage. https://www.conqat.org/. Accessed 01 July 2017
2. GitHub Homepage. https://github.com/. Accessed 01 June 2017

3. Homepage of GitHub API. https://developer.github.com/v3/ Accessed June 01 2017
4. Ahmed, I., Ghorashi, S., Jensen, C.: An exploration of code quality in FOSS projects. In: Corral, L., Sillitti, A., Succi, G., Vlasenko, J., Wasserman, A.I. (eds.) OSS 2014. IAICT, vol. 427, pp. 181–190. Springer, Heidelberg (2014). https://doi.org/10.1007/978-3-642-55128-4_26
5. Beck, K.: Test-Driven Development: By Example. Addison-Wesley Professional, Boston (2003)
6. Beller, M., Bholanath, R., McIntosh, S., Zaidman, A.: Analyzing the state of static analysis: a large-scale evaluation in open source software. In: Proceedings of 23rd IEEE International Conference on Software Analysis, Evolution, and Reengineering (SANER), pp. 470–481. IEEE (2016). https://doi.org/10.1109/SANER.2016.105
7. Bird, C., Nagappan, N., Devanbu, P., Gall, H., Murphy, B.: Does distributed development affect software quality? An empirical case study of Windows Vista. Commun. ACM **52**(8), 85–93 (2009)
8. Bird, C., Nagappan, N., Murphy, B., Gall, H., Devanbu, P.: Don't touch my code! examining the effects of ownership on software quality. In: Proceedings of the 19th ACM SIGSOFT Symposium and the 13th European Conference on Foundations of Software Engineering (FSE), pp. 4–14. ACM (2011)
9. Bissyandé, T.F., Thung, F., Lo, D., Jiang, L., Réveillere, L.: Popularity, interoperability, and impact of programming languages in 100,000 open source projects. In: Proceedings of the 37th IEEE Annual Computer Software and Applications Conference (COMPSAC), pp. 303–312. IEEE (2013)
10. Corral, L., Fronza, I.: Better code for better apps: a study on source code quality and market success of android applications. In: Proceedings of the Second ACM International Conference on Mobile Software Engineering and Systems (MOBILESoft), pp. 22–32. IEEE Press (2015)
11. Deissenboeck, F., Juergens, E., Hummel, B., Wagner, S., y Parareda, B.M., Pizka, M.: Tool support for continuous quality control. IEEE Softw. **25**(5), 60–67 (2008)
12. Deissenboeck, F., Wagner, S., Pizka, M., Teuchert, S., Girard, J.F.: An activity-based quality model for maintainability. In: IEEE International Conference on Software Maintenance (ICSM 2007), pp. 184–193. IEEE (2007)
13. Eisenhardt, K.M.: Building theories from case study research. Acad. Manag. Rev. **14**(4), 532–550 (1989)
14. El Emam, K., Benlarbi, S., Goel, N., Rai, S.N.: The confounding effect of class size on the validity of object-oriented metrics. IEEE Trans. Softw. Eng. **27**(7), 630–650 (2001)
15. Fjeldstad, R.K., Hamlen, W.T.: Application program maintenance study: Report to our respondents. In: Proceedings Guide, vol. 48 (1983)
16. Google: Google Java Coding Guidelines (2016). https://google.github.io/styleguide/javaguide.html. Accessed 02 Oct 2017
17. Gousios, G.: The GHTorrent dataset and tool suite. In: Proceedings of the 10th Working Conference on Mining Software Repositories (MSR), pp. 233–236. IEEE Press, Piscataway (2013)
18. Heinemann, L., Hummel, B., Steidl, D.: Teamscale: software quality control in real-time. In: Companion Proceedings of the 36th International Conference on Software Engineering (ICSE), pp. 592–595. ACM (2014)
19. Heitlager, I., Kuipers, T., Visser, J.: A practical model for measuring maintainability. In: Proceedings of 6th International Conference on the Quality of Information and Communications Technology (QUATIC 2007), pp. 30–39. IEEE (2007)

20. Hönick, S.: How Does the Programming Language Affect the Quantity of Code Clones in Open Source Software? Master's thesis, Technische Universität München (2015)
21. Juergens, E.: Why and How to Control Cloning in Software Artifacts. Ph.D. thesis, Technische Universität München (2011)
22. Kabacoff, R.: R in Action: Data Analysis and Graphics with R. Manning Publications Co. (2015)
23. Kalliamvakou, E., Gousios, G., Blincoe, K., Singer, L., German, D.M., Damian, D.: The promises and perils of mining GitHub. In: Proceedings of the 11th Working Conference on Mining Software Repositories, pp. 92–101. ACM (2014)
24. Kochhar, P.S., Wijedasa, D., Lo, D.: A large scale study of multiple programming languages and code quality. In: Proceedings of the 23rd IEEE International Conference on Software Analysis, Evolution, and Reengineering (SANER), vol. 1, pp. 563–573. IEEE (2016)
25. Koschke, R., Bazrafshan, S.: Software-clone rates in open-source programs written in C or C++. In: Proceedings of the 23rd IEEE International Conference on Software Analysis, Evolution, and Reengineering (SANER), pp. 1–7. IEEE (2016)
26. Martin, R.C.: Clean Code: A Handbook of Agile Software Craftsmanship. Pearson Education, London (2009)
27. Miller, G.A.: The magical number seven, plus or minus two: some limits on our capacity for processing information. Psychol. Rev. **63**(2), 81 (1956)
28. Minelli, R., Mocci, A., Lanza, M.: I know what you did last summer: an investigation of how developers spend their time. In: Proceedings of the 23rd IEEE International Conference on Program Comprehension (ICPC), pp. 25–35. IEEE Press (2015)
29. Nagappan, N., Murphy, B., Basili, V.: The influence of organizational structure on software quality. In: Proceedings of the 30th ACM/IEEE International Conference on (ICSE), pp. 521–530. IEEE (2008)
30. Norick, B., Krohn, J., Howard, E., Welna, B., Izurieta, C.: Effects of the number of developers on code quality in open source software: a case study. In: Proceedings of the ACM-IEEE International Symposium on Empirical Software Engineering and Measurement (ESEM), p. 62. ACM (2010)
31. Ostberg, J.P., Wagner, S.: On automatically collectable metrics for software maintainability evaluation. In: Proceedings of the 2014 Joint Conference of the International Workshop on Software Measurement and the International Conference on Software Process and Product Measurement, pp. 32–37. IEEE (2014)
32. Ray, B., Posnett, D., Devanbu, P., Filkov, V.: A large scale study of programming languages and code quality in GitHub. Commun. ACM **60**(10), 91–100 (2017). https://doi.org/10.1145/3126905
33. Ray, B., Posnett, D., Filkov, V., Devanbu, P.: A large scale study of programming languages and code quality in GitHub. In: Proceedings of the 22nd ACM SIGSOFT International Symposium on Foundations of Software Engineering (FSE), pp. 155–165. ACM (2014)
34. Ruiz, C., Robinson, W.: Measuring open source quality: a literature review. In: Open Source Software Dynamics, Processes, and Applications, pp. 189–206. IGI Global (2013)
35. Samoladas, I., Gousios, G., Spinellis, D., Stamelos, I.: The SQO-OSS quality model: measurement based open source software evaluation. In: Russo, B., Damiani, E., Hissam, S., Lundell, B., Succi, G. (eds.) OSS 2008. ITIFIP, vol. 275, pp. 237–248. Springer, Boston, MA (2008). https://doi.org/10.1007/978-0-387-09684-1_19

36. Samoladas, I., Stamelos, I., Angelis, L., Oikonomou, A.: Open source software development should strive for even greater code maintainability. Commun. ACM **47**(10), 83–87 (2004)
37. Spinellis, D., et al.: Evaluating the quality of open source software. Electron. Notes Theor. Comput. Sci. **233**, 5–28 (2009)
38. Stamelos, I., Angelis, L., Oikonomou, A., Bleris, G.L.: Code quality analysis in open source software development. Inf. Syst. J. **12**(1), 43–60 (2002)
39. Steidl, D., Deissenboeck, F.: How do java methods grow? In: Proceedings of the 15th IEEE International Working Conference on Source Code Analysis and Manipulation (SCAM) (2015)
40. Steidl, D., Deissenboeck, F., Poehlmann, M., Heinke, R., Uhink-Mergenthaler, B.: Continuous software quality control in practice. In: Proceedings of the IEEE International Conference on Software Maintenance and Evolution (ICSME), pp. 561–564 (2014)
41. Wagner, S., et al.: Operationalised product quality models and assessment: the quamoco approach. Inf. Softw. Technol. **62**, 101–123 (2015)
42. Weyuker, E.J., Ostrand, T.J., Bell, R.M.: Do too many cooks spoil the broth? Using the number of developers to enhance defect prediction models. Empir. Softw. Eng. **13**(5), 539–559 (2008)

Author Index

Buchgeher, Georg 125

Elberzhager, Frank 45

Felderer, Michael 33

Halali, Sam 106
Hohlagschwandtner, Markus 95

Juergens, Elmar 151

Kalinowski, Marcos 33
Kieseberg, Peter 14
Kilu, Erki 57
Kirchheim, Konstantin 3
Klammer, Claus 125
Kormann-Hainzl, Gerhard 95

Linsbauer, Lukas 125
Lüder, Arndt 3

Meding, Wilhelm 106
Mendoza, Isela 33
Meyer, Selina 45
Milani, Fredrik 57
Mohacsi, Stefan 73
Moser, Thomas 95

Ochodek, Miroslaw 106

Pauly, Johanna-Lisa 3
Pfahl, Dietmar 57
Pfeiffer, Michael 125
Pölzlbauer, Sabine 95

Ramler, Rudolf 73, 125
Rinker, Felix 14
Roehm, Tobias 151

Salomon, Christian 125
Scherr, Simon André 45
Scott, Ezequiel 57
Souza, Uéverton 33
Staron, Miroslaw 106

Thaller, Hannes 125

Veihelmann, Daniel 151

Wagner, Stefan 151
Winkler, Dietmar 14
Wolfartsberger, Josef 95

Printed in the United States
By Bookmasters